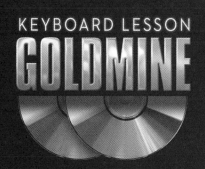

KEYBOARD LESSON
GOLDMINE

100 BLUES LESSONS

BY DAVID PEARL & TODD LOWRY

ISBN 978-1-4803-5481-4

HAL•LEONARD®
CORPORATION
7777 W. BLUEMOUND RD. P.O. BOX 13819 MILWAUKEE, WI 53213

In Australia Contact:
Hal Leonard Australia Pty. Ltd.
4 Lentara Court
Cheltenham, Victoria, 3192 Australia
Email: ausadmin@halleonard.com.au

Visit Hal Leonard Online at
www.halleonard.com

CONTENTS

Lessons 1–50 by David Pearl

Lessons 51–100 by Todd Lowry

LESSON #1: GRACE-NOTE SLIDES OR BENDS

Sliding or bending notes is a concept central to playing the blues. In vocal styling as well as string and wind instruments playing, sliding from one note to another is a standard expressive technique of any blues master. Referred to as both **sliding** and **bending**, this technique involves approaching a note from a pitch either below or above the main note, and sliding or bending up or down to the main note. Piano players are limited in their ability to replicate this because we can't really slide between notes the way a singer or guitarist can, and we can't bend a note flat or sharp the way a horn player can. But we can imitate this technique by playing one or more grace notes leading up or down to a note, and can then create a wide range of sliding and bending options that have come to define blues piano.

Riffs

Let's start with a simple slide up to a note. The example below shows an easy melodic riff, first with no slide and then with a slide.

RIFF 1

TRACK 1
0:00
CD 1

There is no one correct way to play these grace notes: Stylistic interpretation allows for a variety of ways to play. You can play the grace note a bit earlier than the main note, as close to the main note as possible, or even at the same time as the main note. You can release the grace note before playing the main note or release it after playing the main note. Play around with these different methods, and use your ear to choose which style you like. The goal is to develop a flexibility that allows for spontaneous expression.

Here is another melodic riff, then a repetition of the riff with the slide-down technique added. Again, play around with how you articulate these grace notes and their main notes. More expressive possibilities will come out of accenting one or the other of these notes, or tweaking the dynamics of the notes in other ways.

RIFF 2

TRACK 1
0:24
CD 1

Now let's see what other possibilities there are when we add more grace notes. With each added grace note, we lengthen the slide, or make a bigger bend.

Riff 3 puts extra upward slides into the riff from Riff 1.

RIFF 3

And Riff 4 shows downward slides filled in with chromatic grace notes.

RIFF 4

Of course, slides and bends shouldn't be used to the point of excess, but adding these slides up and down will give a bluesy dimension to your playing in many ways.

LESSON #2: GOOD "GOOD" FINGERING

When you're playing blues riffs in the right hand and boogie patterns in the left, you need your fingers to work for you, helping you get the right articulation, the right accent, or the best movement to a new hand position. Good fingering is the key to getting around the keyboard and playing expressively. But good fingering is more than what you may have learned when you were practicing your scales with Mrs. Knucklebuster down the street. It's applying different techniques to what you want to play, how you want to play it, and the individual characteristics of your hand.

Alternate Fingering

This lesson works with a traditional approach to fingering: **alternate fingering**. Alternate fingering means using adjacent fingers for adjacent notes, or alternating between two adjacent fingers for a pattern of notes, in scales or other pattern of notes, while avoiding using the thumb on black keys.

Example 1 shows several alternate fingering combinations for the right hand. Notice how fingers 1, 2, and 3 alternate in different combinations, from 2-3-1 to 3-2-1 to 2-3-1-3-2. Because they are the most flexible and agile of the fingers, they are the best to use in navigating these ascending, descending, and crossover moves.

EXAMPLE 1

Example 2 shows a bluesy bass figure for the left hand, using good alternate fingering, also in both ascending and descending movement. Notice which fingers fall on the beats (1, 2, 3, and 4), as opposed to the upbeats (the "ands"), so you can give these beats more weight while you keep the upbeats lighter. This requires careful planning, keeping an eye out for where the fingers will land on the keyboard.

EXAMPLE 2

Smooth Riffs

Planning your fingering can help you play fast and **smooth blues** riffs up and down the keyboard. In the next example, check out how alternate fingering can facilitate the alternating white and black keys in this bluesy run up and down the keyboard, using the longer fingers (2 and 3) on the black keys and the thumb on the white keys. You should sense a comfortable position for your hand, compact and rounded with fingers slightly curved, easy as it moves up to the right and then down to the left.

EXAMPLE 3

Left-hand boogie patterns are notoriously tricky. The next boogie-style passage for the left hand shows similar alternate finger planning can help you smooth out a tricky passage.

EXAMPLE 4

You can use alternate fingering for passages that call for smooth articulation, in either *legato* phrasing or groups of notes you want to sound even in terms of dynamics. Alternate fingering also is the way to go when planning fast passage work up and down the keyboard.

LESSON #3: GOOD "BAD" FINGERING

Playing the blues really demands a maximum amount of expression. Why would you be playing the blues if you didn't feel blue? One of the ways of expressing yourself through a musical instrument is through **articulation** – the precise way you play a note as defined by its individual dynamic, attack, and release. Put a string of notes together in a phrase and you can easily see the possibilities in terms of articulation in each and every phrase you play.

Non-Alternating Fingering

This unconventional-sounding label fits an unconventional technique: playing two or more notes that are next to each other on the keyboard with the same finger, rather than with alternate fingers. One of the reasons you would choose this approach is because of the sound you get from this deliberate articulation. You can't play two neighboring notes with the same finger and get a true *legato* (smoothly connected) articulation, but you can get a range of detached articulation, from slightly separated to short, *staccato* phrasing.

This first example is a riff in F for the right hand, showing non-alternate fingering applied in a couple of different ways. Chromatic 3rds gain a *staccato* touch from the successive 4-2 fingering, and the three-note chromatic line at the end of the measure gains a heavier, detached articulation from using your thumb on all three notes.

RIFF 1

In the next riff, notice how the non-alternate fingering causes the notes on beat 2 to sound a bit more accented, helping the smoother phrasing to the next note and adding considerable variety to the character of the riff. Notice also how the successive use of the thumb at the end of the riff can still allow for contrasting articulation and dynamics..

RIFF 2

The next riff shows a left-hand boogie pattern in G that benefits from the thumb-to-thumb fingering shown, and contrasts with the smoother articulation of the three preceding notes.

RIFF 3

This walk-up pattern in the left hand, also in G, shows how good use of non-alternate (5 to 5) fingering affects the articulation and keeps your hand in position to manage the wide interval skips.

RIFF 4

Breaking the Rules: Thumbs on Black Keys

A traditional approach to piano technique will have you avoid using your thumb on the black keys when possible. And when navigating a quick or tricky passage that you want to sound smooth, it's best to avoid the extra movement and twisty wrist that can result from having your shortest finger on a black key and your longer fingers going for an adjacent white key in a flow of notes. But when you're playing the blues, you'll want to break the rule to give the rhythm and articulation the right emphasis.

See how having your thumb on the Eb allows you to make these accents stronger, especially because moving off the Eb to the E♮ forces you to return back to the Eb with a dropping motion as the riff repeats and the accents go against the beat.

RIFF 5

And the same with the following left-hand pattern: Using your thumb on the black key allows you to match all the accented notes, beats 2, 3, and 4, in the riff.

RIFF 6

LESSON #4: SLIDING THE THUMB

Playing the blues on piano allows for any number of unconventional techniques. In addition to using the thumb on a black key, discussed in the previous lesson, we can add **sliding the thumb**, literally sliding the thumb off a black key and onto a white key. You can slide the thumb up to a higher white key or down to a lower white key. The situations when you want to take advantage of this technique are when your hand position requires the other fingers to cover other areas above or below the slide, or when the articulation can benefit from the thumb-to-thumb slide.

Let's take a look at some situations like these.

Eighth-Note Slides

This riff for the right hand, in G, slides from an A♯ up to a B♮, and this slide is repeated two more times in the riff. The leap down to the A♯ from the first note, G, causes the thumb to drop a little heavy onto the black key, giving it a harder attack. This is the right way to play it, because it also gives your thumb some momentum as it slides off the A♯ and up to the B♮. So you're going for a nice movement as you slide, with your thumb drawing slightly away from the keyboard as it slides from the black key to the white key.

RIFF 1

The same technique is at work in this next riff, in F, as the thumb slides down this time, making a pattern of black-to-white key slides.

RIFF 2

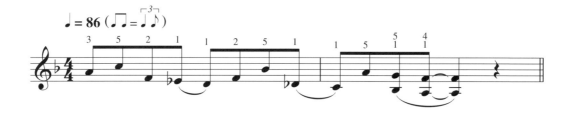

Left-hand patterns make good use of these slides, too, like in this riff outlining a C to F chord progression. When you hit the black key with your thumb, aim for a spot closer to the edge of the key rather than the middle of the key. This way the slide up to the white key involves a short, smooth movement.

RIFF 3

The next riff shows a similar pattern using a thumb slide from a black key up to a white key, but here the context gives extra emphasis on the notes played by the thumb, strengthening the beat.

RIFF 4

16th-Note and Grace-Note Slides

The next riff uses a quick sliding technique, as the black-key grace note is played as close as possible to the main note. Don't be afraid to drop your thumb from just above the D♯ onto the black key, starting the sliding motion as you keep dropping into the E♮ from the D♯.

RIFF 5

This straight-eighth note riff for the left hand, in F, includes articulation to drive the rhythm in an especially percussive style. This time, the left hand does the quick drop necessary to slide from the E♭s down to the Ds, the A♭s down to the Gs.

RIFF 6

LESSON #5: SLIDING THE PINKY

In this lesson, you'll expand your sliding technique, adding the **pinky slide** to the thumb slide you learned in the previous lesson.

Right-Hand Slides

Start out with a riff in G that makes use of the slide up to B from a B♭ a half-step below. Remember to keep the tip of your pinky on the edge of the black key rather than the middle. This way you're in a better position to slide off and into the middle of the B key.

RIFF 1

The next one, a killer riff, relies on careful articulation for a downward slide. Group the slurred notes together and separate the groups so the distinct articulations are audible.

RIFF 2

Left-Hand Slides

Now for some left-hand pinky slides. First try a slide up in this boogie-style pattern in F. The fingering on this is a bit tricky, but practice will prove worth the effort so the pattern becomes comfortable enough to expand into a full 12-bar blues pattern.

RIFF 3

A real workout for the pinky, the next riff imitates a blues guitar pattern that alternates a single-note bass line with upper chord notes in between.

RIFF 4

Quick Slides

Grace-note slides are more difficult, and require nuanced movement in the pinky. This right-hand riff in C features a slide down from E♭ to D.

RIFF 5

Successive combinations of quick slides, both up and down, can be found in progressions like this I-VI-II-V in the key of C. They could be used in a blues turnaround.

RIFF 6

LESSON #6: DOUBLE SLIDES

Double slides are as much fun as they sound, and always impressive to hear and to watch. They are created when you slide from a position with two fingers on two black keys up or down to the white keys a half step away.

Right-Hand Double Slides

In theory, double slides can be created from any interval combination with two black keys. Most common are 3rds and 6ths, with the occasional 4th or 5th.

Our first double slide is in the key of G, a good one for slides resulting from the proximity of F# major and its five black keys just a half step below – perfect for sliding up.

RIFF 1

Next, try these double slides in the key of C. Take a ride on these two downward slides, one on an interval of a 6th and one on a 3rd.

RIFF 2

Back in the key of G, here are some slides that work well in 3rds.

RIFF 3

A double slide on the interval of a 4th may be rare, but it can produce some screeching, wailing magic when taken advantage of. Check out how the slow, 12/8 groove adds to the power of the grace-note slides.

RIFF 4

Left-Hand Double Slides

It's nice to get the left hand in on the double slide action, even though you won't typically do as much riffing with the left hand. This riff takes the double slide introduced in Riff 1 and incorporates it into a left-hand blues pattern.

RIFF 5

Here is a blues pattern that is as familiar as it is irresistible. Make the most of the slur patterns here. The double slide happens just once and is placed right in the middle of the pattern for maximum effect.

RIFF 6

The next riff shows a double slide you can use playing a blues in A. The bluesy sound is from the top note of the riff sliding up into the ♭7th of the key, G♮.

RIFF 7

EASY LEFT-HAND PATTERNS

Playing blues piano is a blessing as well as a burden. With just you and the 88s you can play a complete, satisfying blues, because while your right hand is rolling out the riffs your left hand is laying down the groove and the chord changes. To pull this off, you've got to learn a variety of left-hand accompaniments that become second nature to you so your right hand has the freedom to sing, wail, moan, and riff to your heart's delight. These accompaniments can be learned as patterns – patterns can be transposed to play in any blues in any key using dominant 7th chords throughout the blues progression.

Playing a Pattern Throughout a 12-Bar Blues

Start with a simple, one-measure pattern. This one is made of four quarter notes in the key of G. The four quarters are, in order, G (the root), E (the major 6th above the root), D (the perfect 5th above the root), and back to E (the major 6th above the root). Here's how you put the pattern into every measure of a standard 12-bar blues:

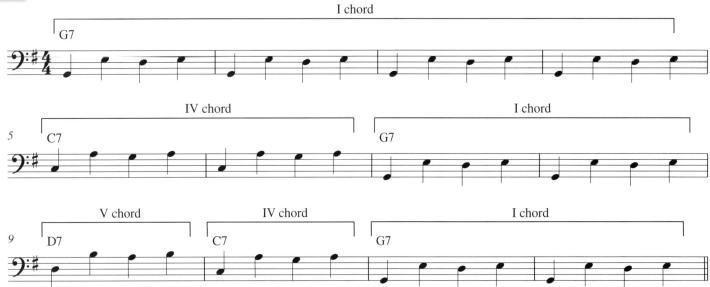

One-Measure Patterns

Take any one of these patterns and put them in a blues progression as shown above. Just follow the rhythm and interval recipe for each one and transpose to the I, IV, or V chord of any key.

Pattern 1 is simple, using only quarter notes. Pattern 2 adds an eighth note to the rhythm, and uses the ♭7th on beat 3 for a bluesy touch. Pattern 3 is a variation on 2, but with eighth notes leading down the scale on beat 4.

PATTERNS 1-3

The next two patterns feature a rest on beat 2, lending a nice skip to the rhythm. These bring to mind the early rhythm and blues of Fats Domino and the New Orleans style. Check out how the triplet on beat 4 of Pattern 5 gives it a rhythmic kick.

PATTERNS 4-5

Two-Measure Patterns

As you learn to drop these patterns into a blues form, you'll see that you can use a two-measure pattern for all but bars 9 and 10 of a standard blues progression. In other words, a two-measure pattern can be used in bars 1 and 2, 3 and 4, 5 and 6, 7 and 8, and 11 and 12. For bars 9 and 10, where the chord changes from a V chord to a IV chord, you can use either the first measure or the second measure of the pattern, whichever you feel works best in context.

These patterns get you into boogie territory, with non-stop eighth notes and repeated notes. Pattern 6 rolls along combining the root, 5th, 6th, and ♭7th of the chord. Pattern 7 fits easily in the hand, and ends with octave eighth notes that break up the pattern and help highlight the two-measure structure.

PATTERN 6-7

Play these patterns at different tempos and see how the feel of the blues can change. Also keep in mind that you can play them with either a swing feel or rock feel by playing swing eighths or straight (even) eighths.

INTERMEDIATE LEFT-HAND PATTERNS

The patterns in this lesson are a bit more challenging than those in Lesson #7, and feature two-note combinations, continuous eighth-note motion, or changing hand position. As with all left-hand patterns, you need to develop a level of comfort so you can keep them "on the back burner" – you have to be aware and in control of them, but they can't take up too much of your attention, which is focused more on your right hand. You'll need plenty of practice to work these into your blues repertoire, but the payoff will be well worth it.

One-Measure Patterns

The first two patterns stick to a basic formula: two-note combinations with intervals of open 5ths, 6ths, and 7ths. These are fundamental blues patterns that require nothing else in providing a solid foundation for some killer blues. Their beauty lies in their simplicity. They leave plenty of room for copious right-hand riffing.

PATTERNS 1-2

Breaking up the 5ths and 6ths in different ways, the next three patterns feature all eighth-note rhythms, amping up the beat quite effectively.

PATTERNS 3-5

The next three patterns all play around with the minor 3rd to major 3rd sound (A♯ to B♮) heard in Pattern 4 above. You'll see that the open 5ths and 6ths, when repeated in eighth-note rhythms, lend a roadhouse blues feel to the patterns.

PATTERNS 6-8

Two-Measure Patterns

Pattern 9 is a classic of early rock, and can be played over a faster tempo with a straight-eighth note beat like that of "Blue Suede Shoes" or "Rock Around the Clock."

PATTERN 9

Now put a little boogie-woogie into the pattern by adding an eighth note in between each quarter note in Pattern 10. Keep in mind that playing all eighth-note patterns like this can be tiring for your hands. Aim to keep a loose, flexible feeling in your wrist, while keeping a solid tone in your fingertips and staying close to the keys.

PATTERN 10

Tip: Try playing these patterns with a simple, repeating blues riff or melody to start out. Something easy, using two, three, or four notes, will do. First play the left-hand pattern all the way through the blues progression, then add your right-hand riff on top. See if you can keep both the pattern and the riff going. Once you can, add more right-hand notes in slow, incremental stages.

LESSON #9: ADVANCED LEFT-HAND PATTERNS

The great boogie and blues pianists like Pete Johnson and Albert Ammons were masters of the instrument, and part of their virtuosity is found in their amazing left-hand patterns. They burn, swing, rock and roll through the most demanding blues, all powered by a rollicking left hand. This chapter introduces you to some of the most celebrated finger-busters. You're taking a step toward blues mastery when you can play the blues over these patterns.

Two- and Three-Note Chordal Patterns

Filling out blues patterns with two or more notes stacked harmonically can imply or make explicit a chordal texture. These examples show a richer harmonic life unfolding within the 12-bar blues, the shifting harmonies creating micro-progressions inside the larger blues progression.

In bar 1 of a blues, where we normally think of playing just a I chord, Pattern 1 makes a I-IV-I-IV progression, and Pattern 2 carves out a I-IV-I7-IV progression.

These two patterns, with their three-note chords chugging along, evoke a barrelhouse style. You've got a fistful of notes here, and moving them through a blues progression brings to mind a steam locomotive. It's a lot of sound and a lot of power!

PATTERNS 1-2

Patterns 3 and 4 incorporate chord inversions. The I chord (G) of Pattern 3 is in second inversion, with the 5th of the chord (D) on the bottom instead of the root. Similarly, Pattern 4 starts out with the 5th of the chord on the bottom, omitting the 3rd (B) but reaching down for the root on all the upbeats as the pattern outlines a I-IV-I-IV progression.

PATTERNS 3-4

These next patterns all add the bluesy sound of ♭3rd (A♯) moving up to the 3rd (B), while outlining a more complex chord progression within the pattern. Here a G diminished chord is implied where the A♯ occurs, forging a new chordal relationship between the I chord (G) and the diminished I chord (Gdim). The chord symbols above Example 7 show the fast-moving progression within a single bar.

PATTERNS 5-7

Pinetop's Boogie Woogie

Pattern 5 is quite similar to one played by Clarence "Pinetop" Smith in his hit, "Pinetop's Boogie Woogie," one of the most popular boogies of all time. It's a testament to his control and technique that Pinetop was able to play the pattern, roll out endless right-hand riffs, and narrate the dance moves to his "Pinetop Strut" all at the same time!

Advanced Single-Note Patterns

The following two patterns are challenging because of the octave positions that move along the keyboard. Pattern 8 is easy to remember, if nothing else, as it moves along the root-3rd-5th-3rd of each chord in the pattern. Pattern 9 is the classic boogie pattern found in the sheet music to "Boogie Woogie Bugle Boy."

PATTERNS 8-9

The next two patterns feature chromatic lines with tricky fingering and hand position changes.

PATTERNS 10-11

Two-Measure Patterns

Pattern 12 is a familiar one, featuring repeated notes and used in both rock and swing feels. The first measure of this pattern can be used in measures 9 and 10 of a blues, where only one-measure patterns work along with the chord change from V to IV.

PATTERN 12

Here is a similar pattern, with alternating octaves up and down the keys, again played with either straight eighths or swing eighths.

PATTERN 13

LESSON #10: WALKING BASS

Playing a **walking bass** in the left hand immediately takes you to the jazzier side of the blues. In contrast to left-hand blues and boogie patterns, walking bass lines avoid strict pattern repetition and instead adopt a freer approach to walking through the chord changes of a blues progression.

Stepping Through the Chord Notes

The best place to start in developing a walking bass is by playing the notes of a chord in some logical, that is to say musical, order. As you'll see throughout this lesson, walking bass lines use quarter note rhythms, changing notes every beat. Just as you'd rarely want to walk in place if you were going somewhere, a walking bass line needs direction, and good lines benefit from an overall direction as you walk through the chord changes.

This first bass line walks along the notes of a C7 chord, the I chord in a C blues. Notice the direction of the line, starting on a low C, walking up the octave in bar 1, descending in bar 2, taking a slightly different journey in bars 3 and 4 as it ascends the octave via a shortcut and makes a longer descent back down to the low C.

BASS LINE 1

BASS LINE 2

You're not limited to just one octave here, as the next example shows. It helps to think of imitating some great jazz bassist, playing lines up and down the upright bass.

Adding Passing Notes

The next step (pun intended) is to add passing notes between the chord notes for a line that uses stepwise motion instead of interval jumps.

See how this next line makes use of notes within the scale (in this case, the C Mixolydian scale, or a C major scale with a ♭7th) to connect the chord notes together in a smooth, stepwise line. Include *some* skips in the line and changes of direction – you don't want to sound like you're just playing scales up and down the keyboard – and go for a melodic approach as you construct a bass line. You'll find patterns in good walking lines, but they're neither uniform nor predictable.

BASS LINE 3

Now watch how adding some chromatic passing notes (notes not in the scale) between the scale notes can make for a jazzier stroll.

BASS LINE 4

Walking Through a Blues Progression

Now you can apply these walking concepts to the 12-bar blues. Here is a walking bass line for a C blues, made up of chord notes, scalewise passing tones, and chromatic passing tones.

BASS LINE 5

Now it's your turn to create some walking bass lines of your own.

LESSON #11: 12-BAR BLUES

The **12-bar blues** is the most common type of blues, the one people mean when they say, "Play me some blues." It's instantly recognizable for its simple form and unique musical language, based on "blue" notes – ♭3rds, ♭5ths, and ♭7ths of a major scale. Historically the blues provided a musical form for expressing woes of love and life using three phrases and three chords.

One Chorus of the Blues

When you play the 12-bar blues, you play a structure called a "chorus" of the blues each time you go through the 12-measure form. Each chorus consists of three phrases, each four measures long, in 4/4 time. Let's name these Phrase A, Phrase B, and Phrase C. Here's how it looks when you lay out this form on a music staff:

EXAMPLE 1

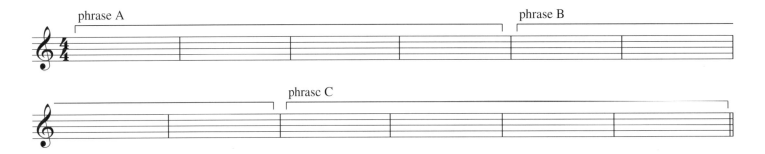

Chord Placement

To accompany these three phrases, you'll use three chords, all dominant 7th chords based on the I, IV, and V of the key. Understanding and internalizing where and how these chords change within each phrase is essential. You'll quickly see how the chord structure gives life to the form, and becomes the heart of the blues. The following example shows the placement of the three chords in a traditional blues.

EXAMPLE 2

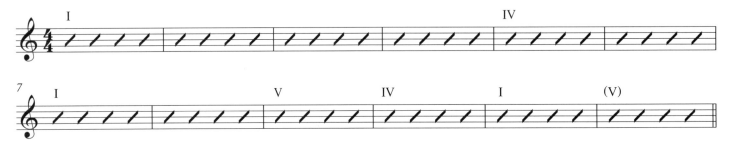

The slash marks in the example above represent beats, one beat for each quarter note. Notice that the chords change on beat 1. The beat is the pulse of the music, and it can be fast, slow, or medium tempo, though a traditional blues is usually a slower tempo. The tempo you set should support the lyrics, the melody, and the rhythmic feel of the blues you're playing.

Repeating the Form

Since one chorus of the blues rarely, if ever, makes a complete song, you can repeat this form, playing three, four, six or more choruses in succession to build it into a song.

In vocal blues a singer performs several choruses, with new lyrics for each. Each set of lyrics is independent, and doesn't have to connect in a narrative way. Instead, vocal blues expresses a condition, a window into a feeling or state of mind to tell a story. A singer will often end a song by repeating of one of the earlier choruses.

An instrumental blues begins with a melody that is built on a riff, or some kind of bluesy melodic motif that can be repeated, with variation, over the 12-bar form. This opening chorus is followed by instrumental solos, improvisations played over the 12-bar form. After the solo or solos, the opening melody is repeated.

Introductions and endings can be added to make a complete, song-length blues.

Three Phrases and Three Chords

The next example shows a complete 12-bar chorus, with a bluesy piano riff in the right hand and a simple blues pattern in the left hand. Check out how they work together to animate the three four-bar phrases and the traditional blues chord progression.

EXAMPLE 3

The **8-bar blues** is probably the second-most common blues form played, after the 12-bar blues. Its shorter form lends itself to nearly unlimited variation and versatility within the 8-bar form, with different versions of the same standard songs by different artists. This lesson covers a few of the most popular versions.

Two Phrases

The 8-bar form has the symmetry of two four-bar phrases as an underlying structure. A graphic representation of the phrases in relation to a musical staff looks like this:

EXAMPLE 1

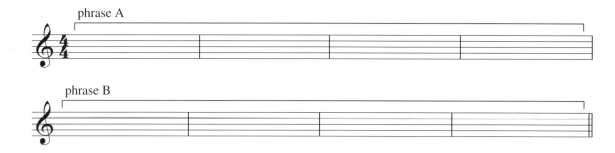

The two phrases work best when the pairing brings out their symmetry, like when the lyrics of Phrase A set up a punch-line response in Phrase B, or when the melody of Phrase A poses a kind of musical question that is answered by Phrase B.

Traditional Chord Progression

This simple and traditional progression is found in songs like "Trouble in Mind" and "Key to the Highway." Like the traditional 12-bar blues, this progression sticks with the basic chords: I, IV, and V of whatever key you're in.

EXAMPLE 2

Swing-Style Progression

The next example shows an 8-bar blues in a style heard in swing and big band hits like the A sections of George Gershwin's song "Oh, Lady Be Good!"

EXAMPLE 3

Stride Blues Progression

Here is another 8-bar progression, this one heard in bluesy songs like "Ain't Nobody's Business." The style here is stride piano, with the left hand alternating bass notes on beats 1 and 3 and upper chords on beats 2 and 4.

EXAMPLE 4

Other 8-bar blues use even different chord progressions, or combine elements of one with another. Both "It Hurts Me Too" and "Cherry Red" use a I-I-IV-IV progression for the first four bars, for example. "It Hurts Me Too" uses the same progression in bars 5–8 of Example 2 above, and "Cherry Red" uses the same chords in bars 5–8 of Example 4 above.

LESSON #13: MINOR BLUES

Minor blues is a blues that uses the form of a 12- or 8-bar blues, but is written in a minor key, with melodies and chords made up of minor scales and modes.

Major-key blues often make use of the "blue" notes – ♭3rds, ♭5ths, and ♭7ths. But just because a melody or riff uses a ♭3rd doesn't make it a minor blues. Flatted 3rds create a wonderful dissonance when played or sung against a major 3rd in the chord progression. Major triads and dominant 7th chords (with major 3rds) are harmonic markers of major-key blues.

12-Bar Minor Blues

A typical chord progression for a 12-bar minor blues resembles that of a major key blues, except the I and the IV chord are minor, and written as i and iv, as follows

EXAMPLE 1

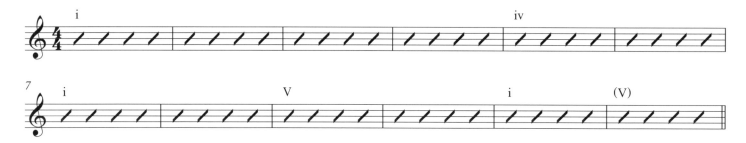

A good example of a minor blues is the song "Why Don't You Do Right?" written by Joe McCoy. It's a 12-bar minor blues with a swing beat that follows this chord progression, with the addition of a V chord on beats 3 and 4 of bar 6.

Common Harmonic Variations

As in all other blues, there are many additions and variations to the basic progression. The next example shows some of the more common ones.

EXAMPLE 2

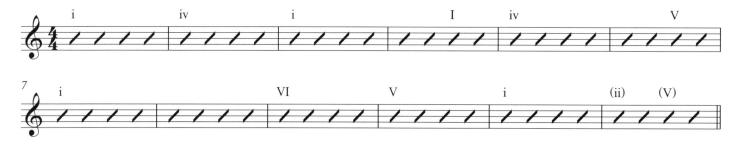

To learn what some of these more remote chords are, build triads on top of every note of the harmonic minor scale for the key you're in. Here are the seven triads built on the D harmonic minor scale:

EXAMPLE 3

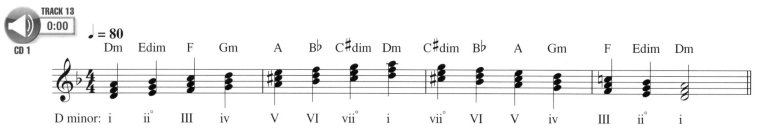

D Minor Blues

To put these chords and concepts into practice, let's make a D minor blues. The next example uses the notes of a D minor triad as an opening riff, and takes it through a 12-bar blues using the chord progression in Example 2.

EXAMPLE 4

Checking Out Minor Blues

The best way to get more minor blues into your song list is by exploring some of the many great songs and styles out there. Here are some suggestions to check out:

R&B

Last Two Dollars (minor 8-bar blues incorporated into a 24-bar form)

The Thrill Is Gone (minor 12-bar blues)

All Your Love (minor 12-bar blues)

JAZZ

St. James Infirmary (minor 8-bar blues)

Birks Works (minor 12-bar blues)

Mr. P. C. (minor 12-bar blues)

Boogie Stop Shuffle (minor 12-bar blues)

Bags and Trane (minor 12-bar blues)

Footprints (minor 12-bar blues in 3/4 time using the Dorian mode)

Señor Blues (minor blues in 6/8 time and Latin rhythms)

LESSON #14: THE FIRST FOUR BARS

The traditional 12-bar blues form is made up of three four-bar phrases, creating a unique and simple form that can be expressed as **A-B-C**, with each letter representing each of the three phrases. Though the form of a traditional blues lyric might be expressed as **A-A-B**, since the second phrase is usually a repetition of the first, musically speaking the second phrase is almost always a variation of the first phrase, not a repetition.

Zoom in to take a closer look at each of these four-bar phrases and you can see the makings of a form-within-a-form. By creating a framework for each bar of each phrase, you provide yourself a specific method for deciding what to play and where to play it.

Phrase 1

A formal representation of the first four bars might look like this: **a-b-a-c**, with each letter representing one bar.

- Bar 1 will be a statement **(a)**, a small theme or riff that can be based on the blues scale, for example, or the notes of the chord, or a combination of the two.

- Bar 2 will be an answer to bar 1 **(b)**, something similar but a variation of the initial statement.

- Bar 3 will be a repetition of bar 1 (**a** again).

- Bar 4 will be the grand finale of **Phrase 1 (c)** – a more emphatic statement that will provide a strong forward push into **Phrase 2**.

Example 1 shows the first four bars of an F blues, with a right-hand line that carries out a one-measure melodic idea through all four measures of an **a-b-a-c** form as described above.

- Bar 1 shows a descending blues riff that uses stepwise motion and descending 3rds that outline an F major chord.

- Bar 2 is a variation – here we'll try something shorter: a condensed version of **(a)**, with the beginning of the statement but a more succinct ending on the ♭3rd of the blues scale.

- Bar 3 is a repetition of **(a)**, with a lead-in to bar 4.

- Bar 4 concludes the phrase. Notice that the melodic line uses elements related to the original statement: a variation of the descending line, but one that starts from a higher pitch (reached by the ascending lead-in at the end of bar 3) and descends more emphatically in stepwise motion.

EXAMPLE 1

Next you can add a simple left-hand blues pattern to accompany the phrase. Example 2 uses an easy, quarter-note blues pattern on the I chord (F) that fits nicely with this phrase.

EXAMPLE 2

Now to add some spice, we'll throw in the IV chord in the left hand in bar 2, a common substitution that adds some interest to the progression.

EXAMPLE 3

So making a great **Phrase 1** of a blues chorus starts by creating an opening riff in bar 1, shaping and developing the riff through variation and repetition in bars 2–4, then adding a left-hand blues pattern that fits the melodic style of the riff and overall phrase.

In 12-bar blues, the second phrase represents the destination of the first four bars. You say where you started from in the first four bars, but the second four bars say where you are going, and what you are going to do when you get there.

Developing Phrase 2 Organically

The melodic material should change in the second four bars, but it must also keep some of its roots from the opening phrase. Harmonically, the blues move from the I chord in Phrase 1 to the IV chord in **Phrase 2**. So the riff should reflect the harmonic change and embody that change in a way that shows growth, taking the idea to a related but different place or mood.

Example 1 shows the opening riff of a blues in F, taken from bar 1 of the first four bars, and how it can be developed – changed to reflect the harmonic change (to B♭7), and then loosened up rhythmically into a new riff for bar 5.

EXAMPLE 1

Let's do the same thing with bar 6: Example 2 shows bar 1 and 2 transformed into bars 5 and 6. Notice the rest at the beginning of bar 6, a new development, and how it takes the riff in a new direction.

EXAMPLE 2

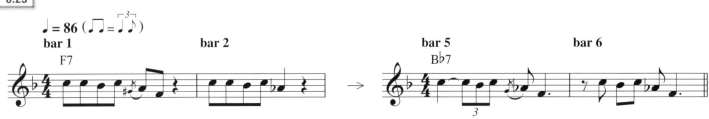

Connecting Phrase 1 and Phrase 2

Now take a look at bars 1–8 in Example 3, comparing Phrase 1 with Phrase 2. In Examples 1 and 2 we developed the opening riff into a new riff for bars 5 and 6 (a & b). In bar 7 (c) this new riff is taken to a temporary resolution, on F. The resolution is then extended to an unresolved note (Eb) in bar 8 (d), as if to say, we're not done yet. Though we've started out in Phrase 1 and gone somewhere in Phrase 2, we are seeking resolution, a new destination, and setting up the third four bars with maximum anticipation.

EXAMPLE 3

To complete the first eight bars, let's add the left-hand pattern started in the first four bars, so we get the full effect of the harmonic change in the second four bars. The harmonic motion moves from the I chord in Phrase 1 to the IV chord for bars 5 and 6, and back to the I chord for bars 7 and 8 in Phrase 2.

EXAMPLE 4

Head on to the next lesson for a look at Phrase 3, and build a complete 12-bar blues.

LESSON #16: THE THIRD FOUR BARS

The last four bars of a 12-bar blues is when you bring it all home, a summary of the pain endured, an accounting of its cost. When you play through **Phrase 3**, you're going for a release, one that you've earned in Phrases 1 and 2.

Function of Phrase 3

The power of the final phrase is found in the chord progression of bars 9 and 10, where one measure of the V chord in bar 9 leads to one measure of the IV chord in bar 10, creating a strong drive to the I chord and the tonal center in bar 11. Keep in mind that this is the only place in the blues where all three chords (V, IV, and I) change every measure.

Example 1 illustrates this driving force, and shows how bar 12 functions as either a turnaround, for repeating the blues form, or an ending.

EXAMPLE 1

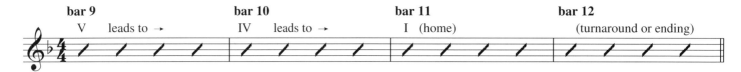

Bringing the Riff on Home

You've introduced a riff in Phrase 1, developed it in Phrase 2, now you want to do something different with it to bring it to its resolution. Keeping things organic, you want to use what you've introduced instead of bringing in something totally new.

Example 2 shows the opening riff from bar 1. Next to it is the riff transformed for bar 9, where the chord changes to the V chord, or C7. See how the riff includes the eighth-note rhythms and bluesy grace notes of bar 1, but the note order is changed, leading up to the C rather than down from the C. This highlights and strengthens the harmony.

EXAMPLE 2

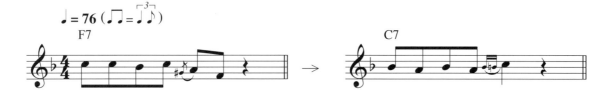

Example 3 shows how the riff develops from bar 9 into bar 10, and resolves going into bar 11. Bar 10 is a near repeat of bar 9, but with an A♭ to match the chord change from C7 to B♭7. Going into bar 11, the riff resolves down to F, in an echo of the opening riff.

EXAMPLE 3

Finishing Touches

Now that we've landed our resolution going into bar 11, we can use the remainder of the bar for a smokin' blues riff to add the finishing touch.

EXAMPLE 4

Now let's put the 12-bars together, with the left-hand blues pattern continuing from Phrase 1 and Phrase 2, and adding a turnaround in bar 12, getting us to the V chord that will lead us into another blues chorus.

EXAMPLE 5

LESSON #17: BLUES PICKUPS

This lesson will help you get the ball rolling with some introductory riffs that set up your blues choruses. Whether you're playing a 12-bar blues, an 8-bar blues, or some other variation, the blues need to be properly introduced. A **pickup** can be short or long, simple or complex. What's important is that you're setting up the key, the tempo, and the rhythmic feel.

The Quick Pickup

The quickest pick is the one that cuts right to the chase. An example of this is the following melodic pickup, only a beat-and-a-half-long. With just an eighth note and a triplet it's a good idea to include a count off if you're playing with a band. This pickup leads into a blues in C.

PICKUP 1

The Bass Line Pickup

Or you could start things off with a bass line in the left hand, establishing the beat and the key as well as the groove, as in this shuffle-style pickup for an E blues.

PICKUP 2

The Right-Hand Riff Pickup

You can rely on a one-measure riff for your pickup, but make sure it's rhythmic enough to establish the beat clearly. The following right-hand riff sets up a driving rock-style blues in A. It's got eighth- and 16th-note rhythms that simulate a drum fill, percussively articulating the beat in bluesy style.

PICKUP 3

Settin' the Groove Pickup

If you're playing in a band, it works well to lay down a solid groove for a couple of bars, enough for everyone to feel the groove so they can join in at the top of a blues chorus. Here is a railroad-style groove in G, chugging along from the get-go.

PICKUP 4

The "Last Two" Pickup

You can go back to the future by stealing two bars from the end of a blues chorus as a pickup. This involves playing something like you'd play for a turnaround, normally in bars 11 and 12 of a 12-bar blues (or bars 7 and 8 of an 8-bar blues). Here's a tried-and-true piano lick that works just as well for a pickup as it does for a turnaround in an F blues.

PICKUP 5

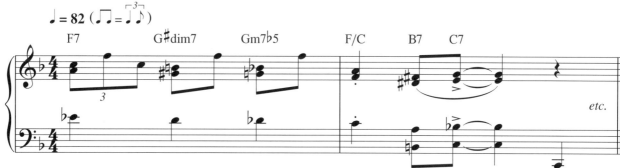

The "Last Four" Pickup

If you need a little more than two bars to introduce a blues, you can always play the last four measures of a 12-bar blues to set things up. If you're into symmetry, you can use the same four bars at the end of the blues as a kind of tag, or coda, making a nice pair of bookends for your blues. Here's an example, starting with the V chord (C7) of a blues in F, and incorporating the two-bar pickup of Example 5, above.

PICKUP 6

LESSON #18: THE TURNAROUND

"It's all in how you get there." Sounds like words of wisdom, right? I'm not sure who said it first, or why, but it sure applies to playing blues **turnarounds**.

The harmonic progression of all 12-bar blues arrives on a I chord in bar 11, and on bar 7 of an 8-bar blues. If you're continuing on to another chorus, you'll be starting on the I chord at bar 1 of the next chorus, so the question becomes how do you get *from* a I chord *to* a I chord. The simplest and most satisfying way is by use of the V chord. But this simple pathway allows for endless variation, and this is where it gets fun.

Basic Turnaround

To illustrate how interesting you can make the journey from I to V back to I, let's take a look at Example 1, which shows both hands playing a single-note descending chromatic line in parallel 6ths in bar 11 of a blues in G. Play these lines and you'll create a sensation both familiar and satisfying.

TURNAROUND 1

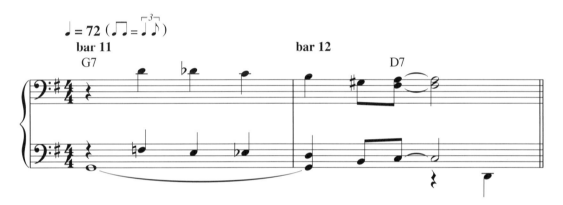

At the beginning of bar 12 you find yourself again at the I chord, harmonically speaking. The line then circles around to approach the V chord chromatically from below.

Developing the Turnaround

Now let's see how we can make this journey from the I to the V even more interesting. Add some eighth-notes to the right-hand part, reaching up to the tonic, G, and back to the descending line, and see what a difference it makes.

TURNAROUND 2

And if that works so well, why not make the eighth notes into triplets and really bring home that blues feel.

TURNAROUND 3

Now you can fill out the sound and get a fully harmonized, bluesy turnaround by adding a note a 3rd below the right-hand part. And in the left hand, you can kick up the rhythm by giving more of a role to the low G, letting it outline the triplets in the right hand.

TURNAROUND 4

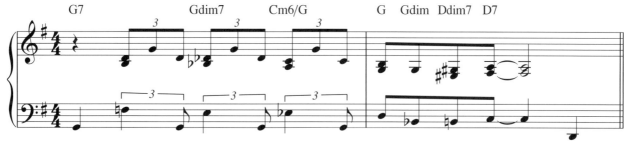

Tip: You can apply this turnaround to a blues progression in any key. Remember to start the line on beat 2 of bar 11, with the right hand starting on the 5th of the home key, and the left hand a major 6th below, starting on the ♭7th of the home key.

LESSON #19: TRIADS

What? A blues lesson in triads? Well, you'll be surprised to find out how many ways you can use a **triad** when you play the blues. And for those who might need to bone up on their diminished and augmented triads, this will come in handy!

Major, Minor, Augmented, Diminished

These four triads can be used with surprising frequency when playing the blues. Complete fluency will prove to be highly valuable. Here is a description of each, in terms of their intevalic makeup, from the root up:

- Major triad: root, major 3rd, perfect 5th

- Augmented triad: root, major 3rd, augmented 5th

- Minor triad: root, minor 3rd, perfect 5th

- Diminished triad: root, minor 3rd, diminished 5th

EXAMPLE 1

Armed with this information, you should be able to construct all four triads in all 12 keys.

Triads in Progression

For an illustration of how easily they can be applied, say you're accompanying a bluesy riff in the right hand with a chord progression in the left. Using only triads and their inversions, here's what you can create:

EXAMPLES 2-3

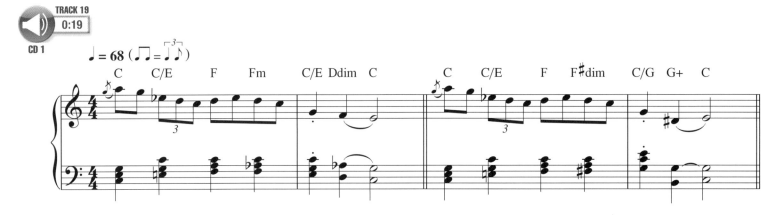

The reason this sounds good is because of the tension you get between the "blue" notes in the right hand (here, the ♭3rd of C) and the notes in the chord. This is important to remember, as it can be the key to getting that bluesy sound when you play.

Harmonizing a Riff

Another application using triads is to take a blues riff, like the one in the next example, based on a C pentatonic scale with an added blues note, the ♭3rd (E♭), and then harmonize it with triad voicings. This produces a superb pianistic sound, full of potential in blues and gospel blues.

EXAMPLE 4

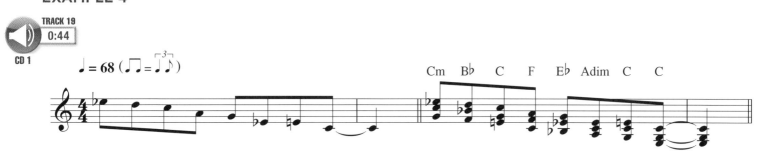

The Blues, with Triads

Putting together several of the elements in this lesson, let's play a blues using only triads in the left hand, following a traditional 12-bar blues progression, with a melody that makes assertive use of the tensions between "blue" notes against the chord notes. And look out for the harmonized riff from Example 4 in bars 11 and 12.

EXAMPLE 5

Dominant 7th chords are the harmonic backbone of the blues. In this lesson you'll examine the inner workings of this blues paragon, and learn to put it into practice in a variety of ways and styles.

The Unresolved Chord

The dominant 7th chord's affinity with the blues is partly due to the chord's makeup, which includes an interval of a ♭5th, or tritone, and an interval of a minor 7th.

EXAMPLE 1

The tritone is the embodiment of unresolved dissonance, a sound that in other musical contexts demands resolution to either a major 3rd or a minor 6th.

EXAMPLE 2

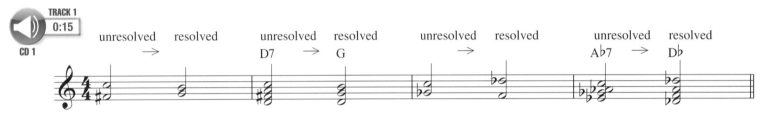

The minor 7th is also an unresolved interval, though not as dissonant. What makes this chord's special relationship to the blues is that instead of functioning as a chord in need of resolution, it is at home in the blues. It doesn't need to be resolved, and in fact its dissonance and unresolved tension is the musical manifestation of the feeling of the blues.

Chord Voicings

As you are mastering a blues, especially in a new key, it's a good idea to take the three dominant 7th chords (the I7, IV7, and V7) through inversions in both hands, to get comfortable and familiar with them. Start in root position and move the bottom note up an octave to play all three inversions, as shown in Example 3. Also, explore some different voicings by dividing the four chord notes between two hands, as in Example 4.

EXAMPLES 3-4

Down-Home Dominant 7ths

Let's see how different voicings can be applied to different blues styles. In Example 5, we'll take the last four bars of a blues in D, and give the V7-IV7-I7 chords a down-home blues style. See how the tritones and minor 7ths are emphasized here.

EXAMPLE 5

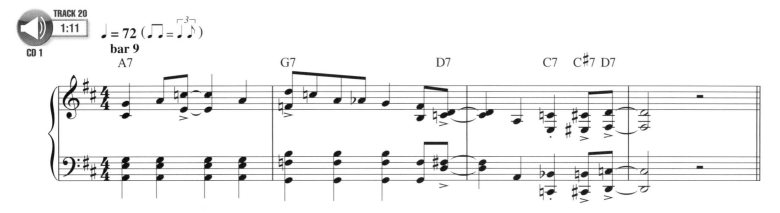

Jazz Dominant 7ths

Because the 5th of the chord is not as integral to the sound of the chord as the root, the 3rd, and the 7th, voicings that omit the 5th sound good, sometimes even better depending on the context. Take a jazz-style setting and you'll see how a lighter, compact voicing works well with the syncopated rhythms to keep things swingin'.

EXAMPLE 6

R&B Dominant 7ths

When you're after an R&B style, use solid voicings that emphasize the 5th of the chord and are played with strong, beat-oriented rhythms.

EXAMPLE 7

No Sweets Allowed?

You may think that major 6th and major 7th chords, with their sweet blend of consonant intervals, have no place in the blues, and you'd be mostly right. Leave it to Steely Dan, though, to find a way to use them: Check out their song, "Peg," which uses a 12-bar blues form with these chords instead of dominant 7ths in its verses.

LESSON #21: BORROWED CHORDS

Hey, neighbor! In life and in the blues, you've got to take advantage of your neighbor's proximity. Rather than feeling limited by only the three main blues chords (the I, IV, and V) you can open up your harmonic horizons by recognizing that each chord comes with its own set of neighbors. Borrowing a neighboring chord is the accepted custom when you're playing the blues.

The Borrowed IV Chord

While you're hanging out on a I chord during a blues chorus, you can add some harmonic movement by borrowing a IV chord and coming back to the I. One of the most well-known blues patterns for piano is a simple I-IV-I shift. Example 1 shows a root-position I chord in G moving to the IV chord (C) in second inversion and back. The inverted IV chord is effective because of the common note shared with the I, in this case the G. Shifting back and forth becomes easy and makes for a great railroad-style pattern.

EXAMPLE 1

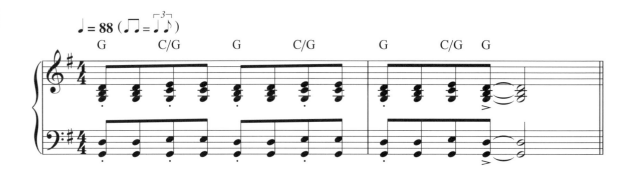

Now take the last four bars of a 12-bar blues in G, and apply this same concept to the V chord and the IV chord, like this:

EXAMPLE 2

Passing Through Borrowed Chords

To take this a step further, you can use the borrowed IV chord to pass from a I chord to a I7 chord, creating a I-IV-I7-IV-I pattern. Example 3 shows this pattern in the key of B♭, and Example 4 shows how you can apply it to the last four bars of a B♭ blues.

EXAMPLES 3-4

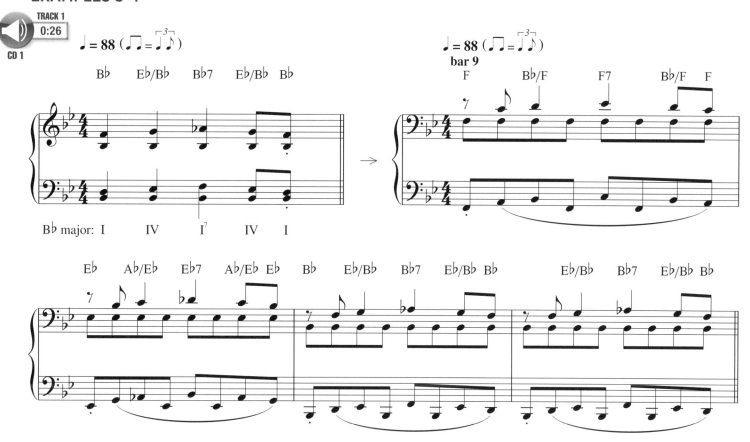

Visiting Other Neighbors

While you're out seeking other borrowed chords, you'll meet up with a few other useful neighbors. Example 5 shows some other neighboring chords in the key of B♭: the ii chord (C minor) the ♭iii chord (D♭), and the ♭VII chord (A♭).

EXAMPLE 5

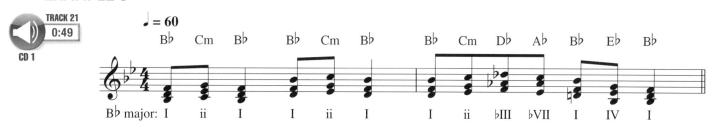

Now see how these borrowed chords can enliven the opening bars of a B♭ blues, with a slow, 12/8 feel that gives you plenty of time to explore.

EXAMPLE 6

Since the concept of using borrowed chords applies to all three basic blues chords, learning them well will prove valuable when you move to other keys that use those chords.

LESSON #22: DOMINANT 9TH CHORDS

If you want to add a little something extra to your repertoire of blues chords, how about adding a 9th? Ninths go especially well added onto dominant 7th chords, and give you a variety of voicing options that open up plenty of stylistic possibilities.

The 9th as Chord Extension

The best way to think about the addition of a 9th to any 7th chord is to imagine it as an extension of the chord. In other words, a dominant 7th is built up from the root and includes the 3rd, the 5th, and the ♭7th. A chord extension adds on to this above the 8th, or octave. So the 9th is nine scale tones above the root. Example 1 shows several 9th chords, with the root on the bottom and the 9th on top.

EXAMPLE 1

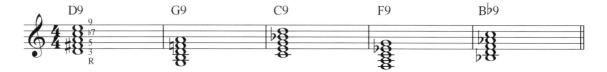

When you count the scale notes from the root to the 9th, you see that it's the same note as the 2nd. As a chord structure, it's best to understand this note as the 9th, extended above the octave. You can also think of the 2nd note of the scale in order to quickly determine the 9th of any chord.

Hearing the 9th

One of the most recognizable uses of a 9th chord is at the end of a blues, when a 9th is added to the final chord, as in Example 2.

EXAMPLE 2

9th Chord Voicings

This five-note chord presents some great opportunities for voicing possibilities. Playing all the chord notes in one hand is possible, but most of the time you'll want to spread the notes out between two hands. Example 3 shows just some of the many creative combinations of a C9 available, not only in distributing the five notes between the hands, but in use of register as well.

EXAMPLE 3

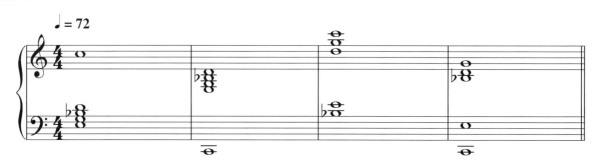

46 100 BLUES LESSONS | KEYBOARD LESSON GOLDMINE

Riffs

You can use 9th chords in all sorts of ways and styles. It can add richness to your traditional 7th chords when you play the blues, add a jazzy lightness to high-register chords, and add bite to mid-register chords.

In a funk-blues setting, 9th chords that are widely spaced throughout the mid-to-high register add the punch of an R&B horn section. Try out these voicings in a funky B♭ blues.

RIFF 1

When you're working in a swing feel, these compact 9th voicings sound great and work especially well if you alternate the main chord with an exact transposition of the chord a half step below or above. Riff 2 shows this in bars 1–4 of a blues in E.

RIFF 2

When you've got a melodic line to play in the right hand, you can divide a 9th chord between the root and the upper chord notes in the left. Riff 3 shows how to do this in a slow and bluesy 12/8 style.

RIFF 3

TWO-HAND CHORD VOICINGS

This lesson takes an in-depth look at different methods to building great **two-hand voicings** that can be used in different styles. Whether you're playing in down-home style, a jazzy blues or funk, you want all the available options at your fingertips.

Heavy/Light Continuum

As you approach chord voicing, it's good to think in terms of how heavy or light their sound is. If you want a heavier sound, choose low-register voicing and double the root and 5th of the chord for strength and support. To achieve a lighter sound, use a higher register, less doubling, and emphasize upper chord notes and extensions that are widely spaced to create a lighter, more transparent sound.

The example below shows voicings of a C7 chord across a continuum of heavy-to-light voicings. Notice the differences in terms of chord inversion, note doubling, and the distance between intervals in these voicings.

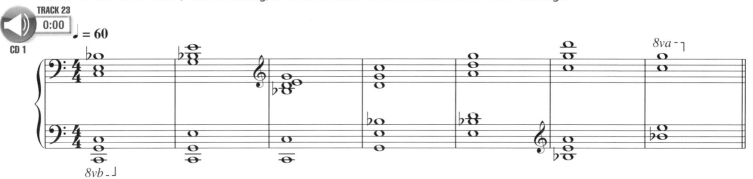

As you study your chord voicings carefully, you'll see the many possibilities that exist when you include the variables of chord inversion, note doubling, and interval stacking. It can be a lot of work scrutinizing all those notes you're playing with all those fingers, and rearranging them to compare the results. But the cool thing about doing this work is that it opens you up to voicings you don't automatically consider, and leads you to new ones you never considered before.

Riffs

Here are examples for each of the seven voicings above, applied to different contexts where they sound good. You'll find that there are quite a lot of situations you'll want to use these voicings. It's good to wrap your mind around them so they're at the ready when you get a chance to use them.

RIFF 1

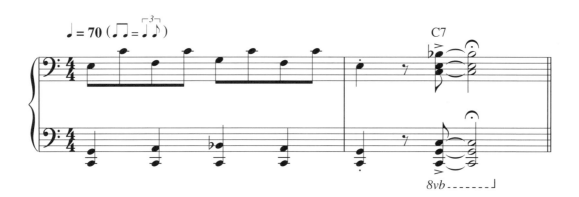

RIFF 2

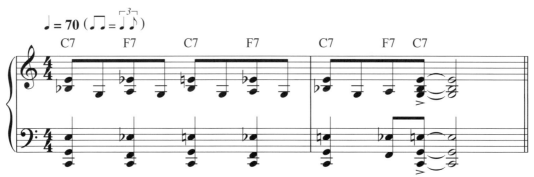

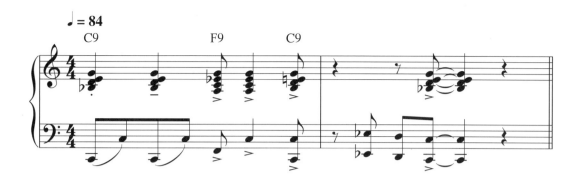

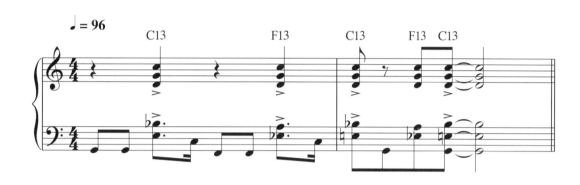

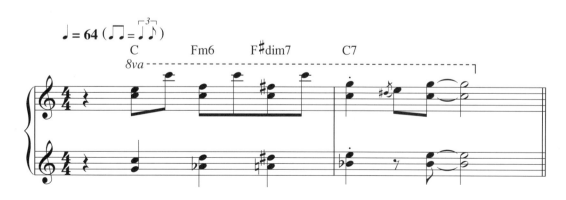

LESSON #24: CHORD SUBSTITUTIONS

Diatonic Substitutions

The three traditional blues chords, the I, IV, and V, are dominant 7th chords built on the diatonic scale of the home key. If you're playing a blues in C, the I chord is a C7, built on the first note of a C scale. Likewise, the IV chord is an F7, built on the fourth note of the C scale, and the V chord is a G7, built on the fifth note of a C scale. The first place to look in exploring **chord substitutions** is in these and other chords built on the diatonic scale. Example 1 shows a 12-bar blues structure with some common diatonic chord substitutions.

EXAMPLE 1

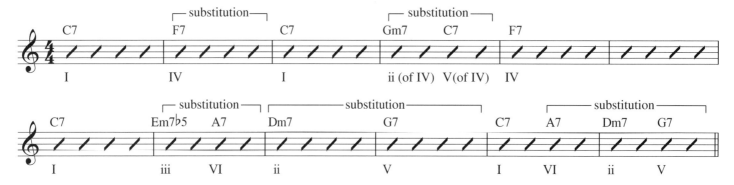

Going in order of appearance, here's an outline of these substitutions:

- In bar 2, you can play a IV chord instead of a I chord.

- In bar 4, instead of playing the I chord, make it a ii-V leading to the IV chord. (Here, the Gm7 is the ii chord of F, and the C7 is the V chord of F.)

- In bar 8, substitute iii-VI for the I chord, which leads you to…

- Bars 9 and 10, where you can substitute a ii-V for the traditional V-IV progression.

- In bars 11-12, you can play I-VI-ii-V instead of the I chord or the I-V turnaround.

- Example 2 shows these substitutions written out in simple voicings. Notice how the substitutions add harmonic movement within the blues structure.

EXAMPLE 2

Tritone Substitutions

Another common chord substitution is called a **tritone substitution**. Whenever you have a dominant 7th chord that leads to a chord a 5th down (as in any V-I progression) you can substitute a dominant 7th chord a tritone away (an augmented 4th/diminished 5th) for that chord. In Example 3 below, the C7 in bar 1 of a C blues leads to an F7 in bar 2. Since an F7 is a 5th below a C7, you can substitute a G♭7 (an augmented 4th down) in place of the C7.

Examples 3–6 illustrate this in several of the places in the blues where you can apply it, showing a chord or chord progression on the left and the substitution on the right.

EXAMPLES 3–6

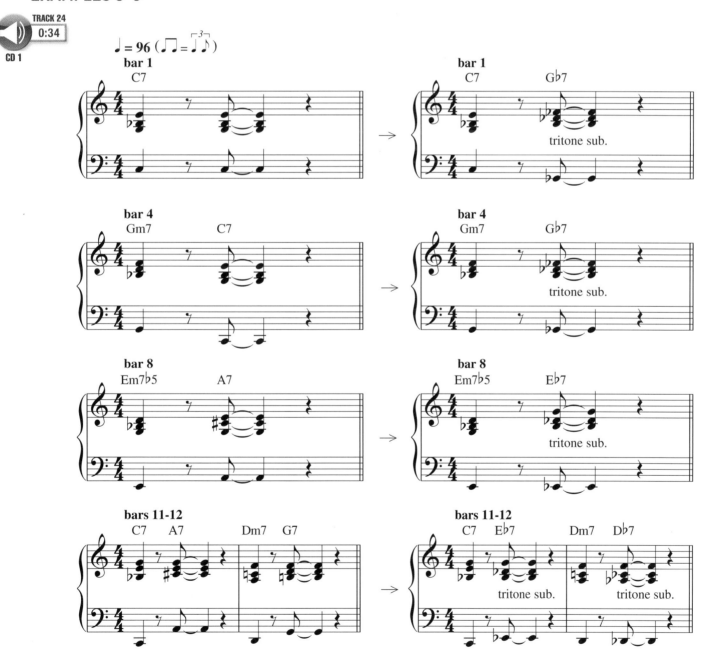

CHROMATIC PASSING CHORDS

Want to learn a fun way to add a little extra grooviness to your blues chord progressions? This lesson shows you how to get where you're going with extra style, by using chromatic passing chords in those progressions.

Half-Step Approach

Here's how it works: Any of the three traditional blues chords (I, IV, or V) can be approached from a chord a half step below or above. Let's say you're playing a blues in G, and are moving from the I chord in bar 1 to the IV chord in bar 2 and back to the I in bar 3. Example 1 shows how you can turn an average G7 to C7 progression (on the left) into something snazzier by using a D♭7 before going to the C7 and playing an F♯7 before going back to the G7.

EXAMPLE 1

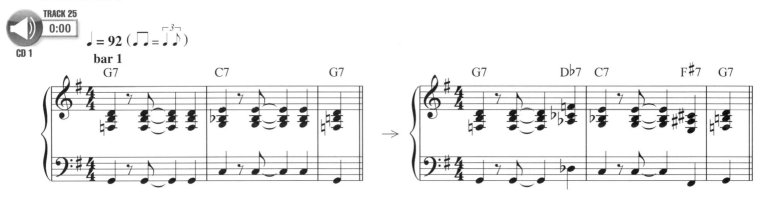

In the same way, the V-IV-I progression of bars 9–11 in a 12-bar blues can be played with added chromatic passing chords. Here is a cool-sounding way to do it in an F blues.

EXAMPLE 2

If you keep in mind that these harmonic passing chords create melodic interest as well as harmonic interest, it will help guide you to know when and where they're best used.

Riffs

Let's take a look at how to incorporate chromatic passing chords into a solo style, where melodic lines are the focus.

This first riff plays with a chromatic melody line, harmonizing it with dominant 7th chords that approach the I and IV chords chromatically, starting from two half steps below, passing through the chord one half step below and then reaching the target chord.

RIFF 1

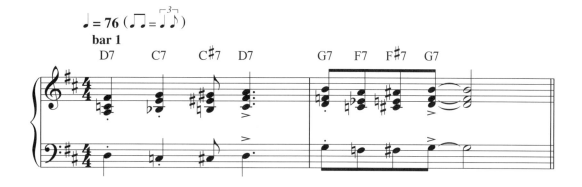

The next riff extends the idea of passing through a series of chromatic chords further, embellishing a melody that takes you through a V-IV-I progression in B♭ with chromatic passing chords

RIFF 2

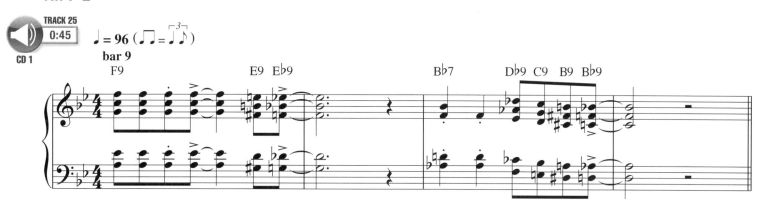

In Riff 3 we'll add more passing chords to Riff 2 and include a turnaround to the V chord in bar 12.

RIFF 3

Obviously, it's a good idea to make sure the situation is right for adding chromatic passing chords – you don't want to start adding impromptu handfuls of them when you're playing with band members who won't appreciate your efforts! But in situations where you've got the space, they're great to call on for an effective way to pass from one chord to the next.

LESSON #26: DIMINISHED PASSING CHORDS

The dominant 7th chords so common in blues progressions have a natural ally in diminished chords. As you're playing the I, IV, and V chords, you can use diminished chords to move from one to another and even when you're hanging out on just one of the 7th chords.

All in the Family

When you take a close look at the dominant 7th chord, you see that it contains a diminished triad in its makeup. Stack up a D7, for example, and you'll find the top three notes spell out an F# diminished triad.

EXAMPLE 1

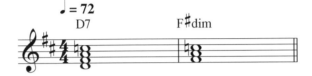

Diminished chords are excellent passing chords because they can resolve any number of ways, including moving to a diminished chord a half step above or below. So it's just a matter of approaching these top three notes in a D7 by a half step below to get this bluesy sounding progression, using a D diminished 7th chord as a passing chord to get to a D7 from a D major triad.

EXAMPLE 2

This use of diminished passing chords goes back to the birth of the blues, and is a signature sound in some of W. C. Handy's compositions, like "St. Louis Blues" and "Memphis Blues."

Riffs

There are plenty of ways of using diminished passing chords in the blues. Let's take a look at some of the ways you can use them in blues riffs.

In Riff 1 we'll take the first four bars of a blues and apply the pattern from Example 2 in a I-IV-I chord progression. Notice how the chord voicings are divided between the hands, with the top note of Example 2 taken by the left hand. This is recreates the sound of a W.C. Handy-style blues.

RIFF 1

Add another passing chord to the progression, and you get another great-sounding piano riff. This time the I-IV progression passes through a borrowed IV chord (G/D in bar 1 and C/G in bar 2) as well as a diminished chord on the way to a dominant 7th chord.

RIFF 2

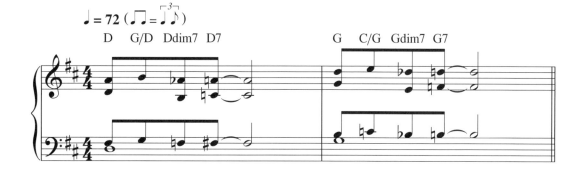

If we extend Riff 2 into bars 3 and 4 of a blues, we could get something like Riff 3, which leads to a D-Ddim-D7 passing chord sequence in the left hand under a smokin' blues fill in the right hand.

RIFF 3

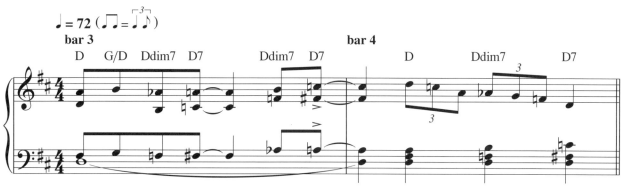

Because they work so well in chromatic movement, you can build a sequence of diminished passing chords leading from one chord to the next. In Riff 4 you can find them leading down and up between dominant 7th chords, this time in F.

RIFF 4

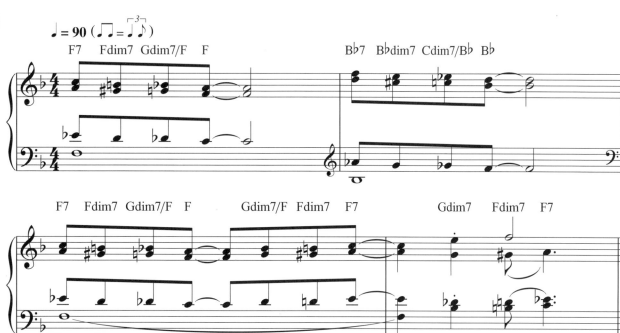

It's a great idea to get as familiar as you can with diminished chords, so you can apply them to blues in different keys and different ways. They are useful passing chords with an inherently bluesy sound.

LESSON #27: ALBERT AMMONS STYLE

Born in Chicago, **Albert Ammons** (1907–1949) was influenced by one of the earliest boogie pioneers, Jimmy Yancey. His background playing percussion helped him develop a strong sense of time and a propulsive beat. Ammons teamed up with fellow Chicagoan Meade "Lux" Lewis early on, and the two later joined with Pete Johnson in New York to become the three pianists to popularize boogie woogie.

Riffs

Ammons had a real affinity for two note combinations in his riffs. He liked to take a riff and harmonize it, for example using 3rds, as in Riff 1. Matched with a two-note boogie pattern in the left hand, it makes for a unique style.

RIFF 1

Riff 2 shows this same approach with 6ths, this time with a rollicking left-hand pattern.

RIFF 2

A more unconventional approach he used was to fill in an octave run with the 5th of the scale in between. He would usually use this in C major, so he could use mostly white keys for the riff.

RIFF 3

He could rock the house with double-handed tremolos. Here's an example of what he liked to do to introduce a boogie.

RIFF 4

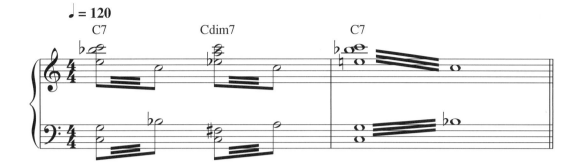

Pentatonic Runs

Ammons could really blaze a trail down the keyboard. He liked to work his way down the C and G pentatonic scales in groups of notes, doubling back at points for a hand position change before plunging down another steep slope.

RIFF 5

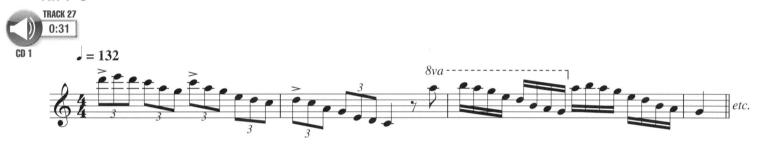

Pentatonic Left-Hand Patterns

His left-hand boogie patterns could be real finger-busters. These eight-to-the-bar patterns show how Ammons liked to work with pentatonic scales in both hands.

PATTERN 1

And for an even more original use of the pentatonic, he would boogie down and up two octaves while outlining a G pentatonic scale.

PATTERN 2

LESSON #28: PETE JOHNSON STYLE

Born in Kansas City, **Pete Johnson** (1904–1967), like Albert Ammons, was a drummer as a youngster and moved to the piano later. He performed with blues man Joe Turner, and did a lot of accompanying as well as solo playing. He performed at the concert *From Spirituals to Swing* in 1938 as part of a three-piano team with Ammons and Meade "Lux" Lewis. He was incredibly versatile and displayed in an incredible range of blues genres, including stride, boogie, and a combination called "rent party" style. His composition "Roll 'em Pete" is mentioned as a possible precursor to rock 'n' roll.

Johnson was a pioneer with riffs that made their way into the vocabulary of rock 'n' roll. For example, he liked to emphasize a syncopation that pushed the beat forward by continually anticipating the downbeat. He'd do something like this:

RIFF 1

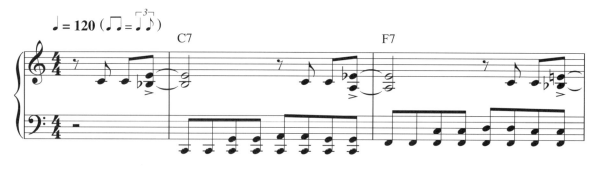

And he loved to repeat a lick over and over, really laying into the beat.

RIFF 2

He could extend a riff into a larger phrase, kicking off a blues chorus from a simple riff, like this:

RIFF 3

Johnson made use of every note in the blues scale, both in his right-hand riffs and left-hand patterns. Here's a blues combo illustrating something he'd play:

RIFF 4

In a slower blues, Johnson would combine elements of stride into his left-hand style. With a wide hand span, it was easy for him to play 10ths, and he mixed in some upper-register triads and lower bass notes in an easy, four-beat feel.

RIFF 5

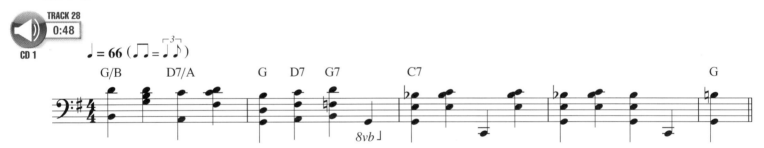

At his rockin' and rollin' best, Pete Johnson would pull out an octave boogie pattern in his left hand, and work a riff into a phrase to end a song. This four-bar ending to a blues in F shows this style.

RIFF 6

JOSEPH "PINETOP" PERKINS STYLE

Joseph Williams "Pinetop" Perkins (1913–2011) was born in Mississippi. He did not write "Pinetop's Boogie Woogie" (that was written by Pinetop Smith), but he played it so well people started calling him Pinetop, too. His roots are in the Mississippi Delta blues tradition, with influences from boogie. Since he lived until the ripe old age of 97, he left a substantial discography, with many recordings from the 1990s through 2011.

Boogie Influences

Perkins played with an encyclopedic knowledge of blues riffs, and many of them bring to mind the guitar, which was his first instrument. Check out this G major right-hand riff, with a typical descending figures that can be rolled down at faster, boogie speeds.

RIFF 1

His left-hand boogie patterns combined alternating octaves with a New Orleans-style bounce, something like this:

RIFF 2

Mississippi Delta Style

As accomplished as Perkins was at the boogie style, he was at home with the slower style of Mississippi blues. Best played as a 12/8 feel rather than a swing style in four, the relaxed rhythmic feel and attention to detailed articulation are key qualities.

The next example shows a riff he might play over bars 9 and 10 of a blues in G, with a variety of careful *staccato* and *legato* articulation.

RIFF 3

Thumb Slide

Pinetop would play a white-key glissando down the keyboard using the nail of his thumb on the keys. What he would do to prepare it is to play the note where the glissando starts with his thumb first, getting his thumb in position. Here's an example of how he did this. Notice how he doesn't really strike the G at the beginning of the glissando. It's just where he starts the gliss down.

RIFF 4

In a low-down blues in F, he might play a right-hand riff all the way down in the bass register, bringing a blues chorus to a conclusion.

RIFF 5

His two-handed style in these slower blues allowed for simpler left-hand parts, usually single-note lines that lay down the rhythm. With the focus off the left hand, you can pour your mojo into the bluesy riffs, like this one:

RIFF 6

And here's a turnaround for a slow, 12/8 blues in G, à la Pinetop Perkins.

RIFF 7

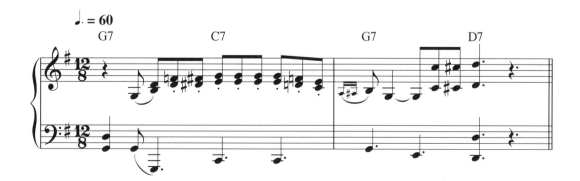

MEADE LUX LEWIS STYLE

Like his fellow Chicagoan Albert Ammons, **Meade Lux Lewis** (1905–1964) was influenced by the boogie pioneer Jimmy Yancey. Lewis developed a big, brawny piano style, playing fistfuls of notes and chords, and a pounding, rhythmic bass. In fact his powerful style shows clear roots of rock 'n' roll, a fact made surprisingly clear by listening to his recordings. In his mid-20s, he recorded "Honky Tonk Train Blues" (1929), and the evidence is already there.

All Aboard!

Let's start with this big phrase for the last four bars of a G blues with a railroad left-hand pattern, and fat, syncopated chords in the right. Lewis could keep this full style going chorus after chorus.

RIFF 1

TRACK 30
0:00
CD 1

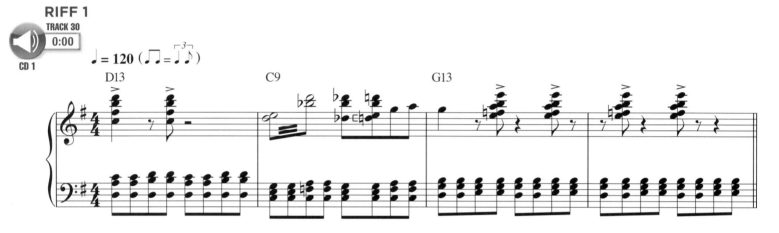

Notice the big, five-note voicings, the dissonances created by the harmonic exploration of the 9th and 13th chords.

Rockin' Riffs

His yen for repeating licks in rhythmic cycles presages a lot of the solo riffing that still goes on in rock today. Here are a couple of patterns similar to those he liked to play. The first uses 6ths in a triplet setting, the second is a single-line riff on a G pentatonic with an added "blue" note.

RIFFS 2-3

TRACK 30
0:12
CD 1

Lewis anticipated rock styles, but also jazz. Take a look at this proto-bebop riff in C that shows his way of circling around a target note using both wide leaps and close chromatic neighbors, the way Charlie Parker would later play on his sax.

RIFF 4

TRACK 30
0:25
CD 1

He brought a novel approach to his left-hand boogie patterns, and always played with a hard-driving beat.

RIFFS 5-6

Lewis could conjure the sound of an entire big band, playing "shout" choruses, where the syncopated hits in the right hand push and pull against unflagging boogie rhythms in the left hand.

RIFF 7

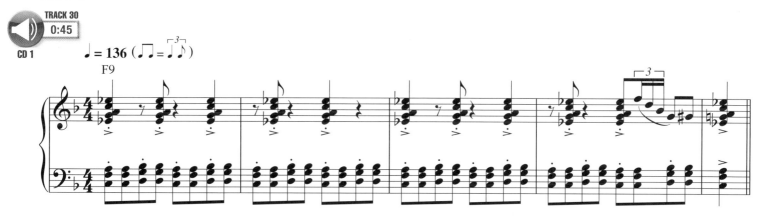

Here are some Lewis-style tremolo 3rds, leading to a classic boogie resolution that takes advantage of the major and minor 3rd in the blues.

RIFF 8

In 1938, the jazz producer John Hammond put on a concert in Carnegie Hall called *From Spirituals to Swing*. The concert featured some of the biggest names in blues and boogie, including pianists Meade Lux Lewis, Albert Ammons, and Pete Johnson. The concert aimed to present the historical sweep of African-American music, from spirituals through ragtime and blues to swing, and was dedicated to the great blues singer Bessie Smith. Lewis, Ammons, and Johnson ignited a boogie-woogie craze that lasted into the 1940s and boosted their careers.

LESSON #31: OTIS SPANN STYLE

The great blues pianist **Otis Spann** (1930–1970) played with Muddy Waters in the 1950s and '60s. His style reflects the slow, bluesy Delta style of his native Mississippi, mournful and sad. He played intimate solos that would draw you in, putting you up close to hear the intricacies of his riffs, every breath and sigh.

Two-Note Riffing

Spann played two-note riffs in his right hand, often keeping the top note the same and putting the melodic movement in the bottom voice. He'd play something like this in a C blues, over the IV chord (F7):

RIFF 1

8-Bar Blues Turnaround

Catch Otis playing an 8-bar blues and you'll take a peek into his thinking. He liked to combine blues riffs that emphasize the minor 3rd and ♭7th, yet sneak in melodic lines that clearly outline the major 3rds of the chord. He really throws light on the chord changes this way, as in this I-VI-II-V turnaround in a C blues.

RIFF 2

Fast Riffs, Slow Blues

Even if the tempo was achingly slow, it allowed him to play fast riffs, and get in all he had to say in the space of a bar of 12/8 time. He liked to make the V chord into an augmented triad, rolling over the three-note chord in a fast arpeggio-like riff, something like this:

RIFF 3

Or check out this fast riff using the notes of a C blues scale, fast and repeated for emphasis.

RIFF 4

Two-Handed Tremolo

Showing some amazing two-handed action, Spann would get going with a two-handed tremolo on a C7 chord, first with the left hand below the right and then switching positions so the left hand was in the middle voice of the chord. This tremolo-style shows the influence of earlier boogie pianists.

RIFF 5

Spann's Last Four Bars

Now let's take a look at his full style. Here is something Spann might do with the last four bars of a blues in D. In the left hand he's got a railroad boogie pattern going, but here the pace is slow, with a detached touch. In the right hand he plays with pentatonic riffs on all three chords (A7, G7, and D7) and injects "blue" notes into them.

RIFF 6

Things weren't always blue when Spann was at the piano, and he would let some sunlight in with a swingin' blues in 4/4 time. Here's an intro riff in G, similar to what he'd play in such a setting.

RIFF 7

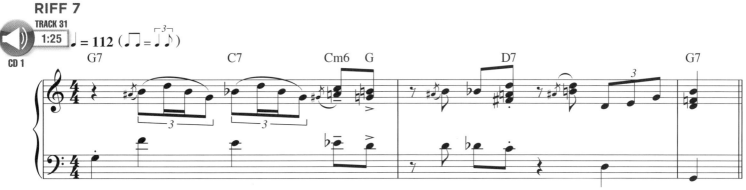

LESSON #32: PROFESSOR LONGHAIR STYLE

Professor Longhair (1918–1980; born Henry Roeland "Roy" Byrd) is all about feel – the combination of rhythms that come together in his style. His piano style is steeped in the melting pot of New Orleans, and he is one of the most important of the New Orleans pianists. In addition to influencing Dr. John, his rhythmic style is found in some of Fats Domino's big hits, which became important in the development of early R&B and rock 'n' roll.

Calypso Beat

Let's start out with the underlying beat. Professor Longhair's style rests on a calypso beat: a syncopated rhythm with a straight-eighth note feel that is captured in the bass line played by the left hand. He plays this calypso pattern or a variation of it in most of his songs.

Now let's look at how he complements this pattern with his right hand. A consistent element of the Professor's playing is that he covers nearly every eighth note in a measure by alternating rhythms in his hands. It's a style that is percussive in nature because it reflects the way you would play a set of bongos or tap out a rhythm on the drums. Start with the following pattern, which shows alternating rhythms in the right and left hands, and practice it until it flows smoothly and naturally.

RIFF 1

Right-Hand Riffing

Next we'll examine the intricacies of his right-hand riffing. There are three elements he plays with: 3rds, fast blues riffs, and chromatic single-note lines. A reduction of these elements follows, formalized into a pattern over an 8-bar blues. This chord progression is one he used in some of his biggest hits, like "Tipitina."

RIFF 2

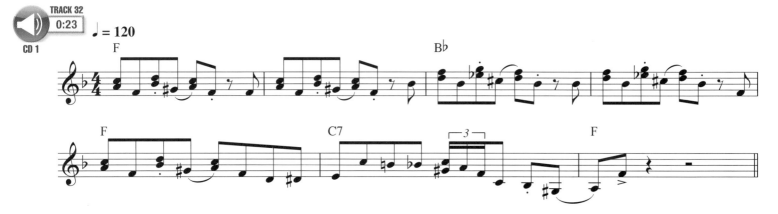

Variations

The next step is to see what kind of variation Professor Longhair gets out of these building blocks. In a slower groove, he likes to play 16th notes in the right hand to layer a syncopated double-time feel onto the calypso bass line.

RIFF 3

And with a faster tempo, he'll expand the calypso bass line into a two-bar pattern, keeping the same syncopated rhythm in both bars. With a more aggressive beat, he'll accent these syncopations to drive the beat harder.

RIFF 4

The New Orleans Style

For an example of how he incorporates everything into an 8-bar form, check out the next example. Here is a variation of the calypso pattern in the left hand, expanded into a two-bar pattern for rhythmic variation. The right-hand part plays in between the spaces in the left-hand part; every eighth note is accounted for. Put it all together, add some bluesy grace note slides, and see how the syncopated rhythms make it dance.

RIFF 5

LESSON #33: DR. JOHN STYLE

Dr. John – look him up as Mac Rebennack, too, because he has recorded some outstanding tracks under his real name – developed his style listening to Professor Longhair and other New Orleans pianists, creating his own stew of blues, boogie and New Orleans funk. Dr. John (b. 1940) synthesized these styles in his playing, and transformed them into a rich and full solo style that raised the bar and moved it forward into modern times.

Right-Hand Riffs

Dr. John operates from a wide-open octave position in his hands, and a lot of his riffs fill in the octave with 3rds ornamented with notes from the blues scale – ♭3rds, ♭5ths, and ♭7ths. Here's an example, working from a C major chord in second inversion and incorporating the bluesy bite when the E and D♯ (or E♭) share such close quarters.

RIFF 1

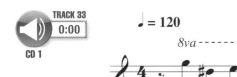

This next riff shows how he can cover a lot of territory quickly, again making good use of ♭3rds and ♭7ths, this time over an F7.

RIFF 2

Left-Hand Grooves

When he decides to boogie down, he uses classic boogie patterns and dresses them up with harmonized 3rds. He plays a lot of his boogies with a straight-eighth note feel, like this one.

RIFF 3

Expanding his left-hand position into wide 10ths, he slides his second finger off a black key and down to a white key for rhythmic complexity in his accompaniment patterns.

RIFF 4

Octaves and 10ths

When you put together the wide spans in both hands, you get a big, harmonically sumptuous sound. Here's an example of his style in a section from a slow, 8-bar blues. Feel free to roll the chords with octaves, 9ths, and 10ths.

RIFF 5

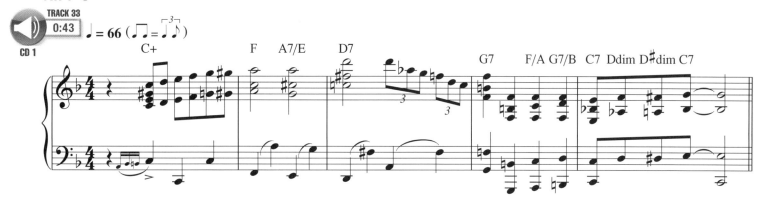

Full-Chord Turnarounds

Even in turnarounds Dr. John loads up the fingers with grace note slides, full chords, and rhythmic power. Here's something he'd do in bars 11 and 12 of an E♭ blues.

RIFF 6

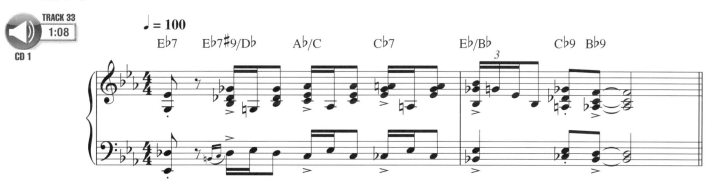

Bring on the Funk

Showing his debt to Professor Longhair, the Doctor raises him one with some New Orleans-style rhythmic funk. He takes the idea of alternating hand drumming to the land of funky 16ths, as addictive to play as they are to hear. Practice keeping the rhythms crisp and clear, making sure each note is audible in the pattern; absolutely no pedal.

RIFF 7

LESSON #34: RAY CHARLES STYLE

As a blues singer alone, **Ray Charles** (1930–2004; born Ray Charles Robinson) stands high among the blues gods for his breadth of work and deep expression. When combined with his piano skills he was unmatched, and he still has the fans to prove it. The way he went about playing the piano is not that hard to understand, but the quality of what he played, his rhythmic feel, and his expressive range continue to make him a favorite of musicians and non-musicians alike.

Ray Charles was successful with audiences of all types. He made it seem easy to cross styles, whether to jazz, country, rock, or R&B. Since blues is the common denominator with most popular music of the 1930s onward, Charles's music represents and reflects the branching out of the tree from its roots. Born in 1930, he became an ambassador to the music world.

Riffs on the Blues Scale

The first thing you notice when you listen to Ray Charles is that his right-hand blues licks are independent of the chord he plays in the left hand. For example, he will play the notes from an F blues scale over a C7 in the left hand. For some pianists, playing notes that seemingly clash with the notes of a C7 may seem unusual, but it's all blues when Ray Charles is playing.

RIFF 1

An important element in his blues riffs is the rhythmic variety he employs. He likes to mix complex rhythms – triplets and 16ths – in unusual and unpredictable combinations. This riff in A♭ shows this variety.

RIFF 2

Jazzy Chords

The influence of jazz is evident mostly in his left-hand chord voicings. He likes to use three-note voicings that leave off the chord root and include the 3rd, the 7th, and chord extensions like the 9th and the 13th.

Above the left-hand chords, he likes to play with octave position riffs, often descending on a blues riff based on the blues scale of the key. For example, in D♭ he would play something like this.

RIFF 3

Down-Home Style

In a slow 12/8 feel, he keeps the same formula: three-note chords in the left hand and octave position riffs in the right hand. Here's a two-bar intro going into bars 1 and 2 of a 12-bar blues in G showing the Ray Charles style. He likes to play with half-step modulations, as in this G13-to-A♭13 progression that he'll use for an opening riff.

RIFF 4

R&B Style

In an R&B setting he liked rolling bass lines with mostly eighth notes, and layering blues riffs in the right hand over a three-note chord in the left. There is always the presence of ♭3rds and ♭7ths, giving a clear sense that his music is grounded in the blues.

RIFF 5

LESSON #35: JELLY ROLL MORTON STYLE

Jelly Roll Morton (1890–1941) was born Ferdinand Joseph LaMothe. His syncopated stride style merged ragtime and blues, and added rhythmic influences from his Creole background in New Orleans. His 1915 composition "The Original Jelly Roll Blues" includes a 12-bar blues form, with a turnaround, and stands as one of the earliest examples of the blues in published sheet music. He takes his place among the great bandleader/pianists in jazz, alongside Scott Joplin, Duke Ellington, Count Basie, and many others.

Right-Hand Filigree

Jelly Roll's right-hand lines were stylish and refined, a characteristic that contrasted nicely with the bluesy feel of his left-hand rhythms. Riff 1 shows a florid passage in E♭ that makes use of his common devises: chromatic passing tones, triplet turns, an overall artistic shape with elegant curves.

RIFF 1

TRACK 35
0:00
CD 1

He would often harmonize his right-hand lines by adding a drone note above the melody, so that the bottom voice played the melody and the top voice played the harmony. The copious use of grace-note runs and tremolos is also one of Morton's calling cards.

RIFF 2

TRACK 35
0:09
CD 1

Ragtime-Stride Combo

The left-hand part is where you see how Morton combined elements of ragtime, blues, and stride in his playing. As the next riff shows, he would break up the traditional ragtime style by adding syncopation and moving lines, like the 6ths leading from bar 3 into bar 4 in Riff 3.

RIFF 3

TRACK 35
0:19
CD 1

He also brought what he called the "Spanish Tinge" to his left-hand parts, a rhythm with a hint of the syncopated beat in fashion in Latin-American countries at the time. Traceable to the *habañera* and the *tango* (but importantly a rhythm of African origin), it brought a new, danceable movement to the blues that would later be developed by other New Orleans pianists like Professor Longhair and Dr. John. It also ushered in an inter-breeding of jazz and Latin music that continues today. Here is an example of how he combined rhythm and blues.

RIFF 4

He established syncopation as the basis of his left-hand accompaniment in many of his compositions, blending ragtime, blues, and stride into a style all his own with patterns like this next one.

RIFF 5

Jelly Roll also arranged music for his group, The Red Hot Peppers, and his solo style reflected his skills as an arranger. Listening to his piano playing you can hear the strumming of the banjo, the sweet clarinet fills, and the trombone entrance all projected onto the 88s.

RIFF 6

JAY McSHANN STYLE

Jay McShann (1916–2006) personifies the Kansas City style, bringing boogie and blues into the jazz era. Playing along with Charlie Parker in his Kansas City band, he infused the blues with elements of swing and bebop, building on the history of what had come before. He was a versatile pianist and band leader, and his ability to call on stride, blues, boogie, swing, and shout styles gave him a strong base to build on.

3rds and 10ths

One of the most prominent elements of his right-hand solo style is his use of 3rds. This first riff shows how he liked to pack 'em in, here over bars 1–4 of an E♭ blues.

RIFF 1

He would feature 3rds in the right hand and 10ths in the left, creating a nice, full sound at the piano. Here is an example, an intro to a "shuffle feel" blues in C.

RIFF 2

Showing the Way to Bebop

Playing with greats like Charlie Parker and Ben Webster must have influenced him to master some speedy riffs. He could play 16th- and 32nd-note bebop fills with the rest of them, like this one in B♭, played with swing 16ths. Notice the chromatic approach to the chord notes – a sure sign that "Bird" was here.

RIFF 3

Big Piano Sound

McShann created some beautifully moving lines using counterpoint. The next example shows how he could work with lines in contrary and parallel motion, with a passage that leads from the I chord to the IV in a C blues.

RIFF 4

And he got a big sound with a full chordal style, packing in chord notes. He would use octaves in the right hand and 10ths in the left hand, and fill them in with juicy chord notes. Here's an example, this time going from the I chord to the IV in G.

RIFF 5

Boogie Woogie, Here I Come

Showing his boogie roots, McShann could lay down the left hand with alternating octave boogie pattern. Here's something he might do with the last four bars of a Kansas City-style swingin' blues, in G.

RIFF 6

DAVE ALEXANDER STYLE

Dave Alexander's style grew out of the down-home Texas blues style. Unlike many other blues pianists he lived and worked mainly in the West – early on in his hometown of Marshall, Texas and later the coast of California. Alexander (1938–2012) changed his name to Omar Khayam in 1976, and recorded under the name Omar Sharriff (or Shariff). He was influenced by Lloyd Glenn, another pianist from Texas who made his career in California.

Stride and Harmonized Blues Licks

Alexander liked to play a slow, 12/8 style of blues, with plenty of riffs tinged with "blue" notes. His left hand would vary a stride pattern, alternating bass notes and mid-register chords. In the right hand he liked two-note riffs in the style of Jelly Roll Morton, with the lower note playing the main melodic riff and the upper note providing a harmony. Here is an example of this style, using a 12/8 blues in C. Notice the use of the augmented chord on the V (G7+), one of his favored chords.

RIFF 1

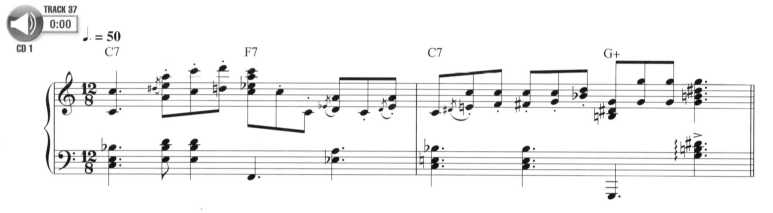

He expanded on this technique of putting the melody in the lower voice in the right hand, sometimes playing two- or three-note chords above the melodic line. He also developed the stride style to incorporate a bit of boogie by adding a melodic bass riff to the lower bass notes of the stride style. Here's what this elaborate style sounded like, in bars 9–12 of an F blues.

RIFF 2

Tricks of the Trade

Alexander used an effective pianistic trick where he'd play staccato chords in the upper register of the piano with his left hand, while his right hand played fast riffs, tremolos, and runs both above and below it. It went something like what you see in Riff 3 at the top of the next page.

RIFF 3

He also played a type of Western Swing where the left hand played *staccato* chords on all the offbeats. The right hand then plays on most of the downbeats, so the boogie-like "eight to the bar" is felt from the combined eighth notes in two-handed style. The relationship to boogie is felt in the constant chugging of the beat, but it's lighter and works well at faster tempos. Here is something like what Dave would do on a minor 8-bar blues. Notice the use of the minor v chord here, another country blues characteristic.

RIFF 4

Blues Bass Lines

Another way he got the Texas style blues going in his solo playing was with a boogie pattern in the left hand. This one uses the root of the chord as a pickup note to the upper voice, which moves melodically from the 5th to the 6th to the 7th of each blues chord. Because the root is never on the downbeat, it has a lighter feel than a barrelhouse pattern, for example. Here is how the pattern sounds over bars 9–12 of a blues in G.

RIFF 5

To get the feel of a bass laying down a bluesy line, Alexander would play a walking bass line pattern in the low register with his left hand, adding percussive chords, glissandos, and shaking out fast chord arpeggios in the right. He kept the quarter-note bass line solid and strong, and that gave him the support to add on these *ad lib* fills.

RIFF 6

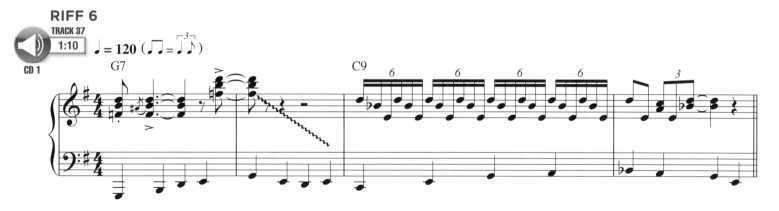

LESSON #38: STOP TIME

Stop time is a musical way of breaking up the rhythmic motion of blues choruses by inserting stops at the beginning of a chorus to feature a solo vocal or instrumental fill. It has origins in ragtime and boogie, where it was used as a break, or stop, in the stride or boogie accompaniment pattern, lasting usually four bars before resuming again. It gives the illusion that time has stopped, but as you'll find, it in fact does not. Read on to see how and why.

Getting Into Stop Time

Stop time usually occurs during bars 1–4 of a blues. "Time" in this context means the beat of the music and the rhythmic content you give to the beat when you play. When you play stop time, the beat doesn't stop – in fact it's extremely important to keep the beat going in your mind and in your body, for example by tapping your foot. But the expression of *playing* time stops. If you're playing a blues pattern, a boogie pattern, a walking bass, or comping, you will stop on beat 1 of bar 1, playing a downbeat note or chord. The sudden open "space" for the remaining beats in the measure can be filled by playing solo fills or riffs, either by you or another band member.

Here's an example of bars 11 and 12 leading into bars 1 and 2 of a stop-time blues chorus in F.

EXAMPLE 1

Beat 1 of bar 1 is punctuated by an accented chord, which serves as a marker for where stop time starts. The solo fill starts on beat 2 and continues into bar 2. The two-bar phrase length is a deliberate choice, as it sets up what to expect in bars 3 and 4, but the phrase length and content is up to you as a soloist and can go in many different directions.

Filling in a Stop-Time Section

Continuing on from where we left off, the setup in bars 1 and 2 leads to the expectation of the following example, which fills in bars 3 and 4 with an answer to the first phrase, and also lasts two bars.

EXAMPLE 2

You see that there is a repeat of the chord punctuation on beat 1 of bar 3 in the left hand. This is optional, but it helps to mark the beat, which continues despite not being played! And it urges on the next phrase, a kind of shout-out that says, "More!"

Adding Variations

You can do more with the punctuation on beat 1 of bar 3 by adding a bass fill leading into it, and adding your right hand to the chord in between the two phrases, as follows.

EXAMPLE 3

Out of Stop Time, Into Time

Stop time can continue for an entire chorus, with punctuations used to outline the form and chord changes, but very often time resumes in bar 5, and you continue with your normal accompaniment pattern as your solo continues. When you're heading into bar 5 in this way, you can tailor your fill to make the most of it. Example 4 shows two ways you can do this. First, let your solo phrase lead into the next four bars of the blues, with the change to the IV chord in mind. Second, add a fill in the left hand like the one here – a walkup to the IV chord, B♭7.

EXAMPLE 4

Stop time is used to great effect in a variety of situations. Singers love to use stop time in many blues tunes, like on the third chorus of "Kansas City" ("I might take a plane, I might take a train…"). Tap dancers routinely incorporate stop time to highlight their fleet footwork.

LESSON #39: TRADING FOURS

The concept of **trading fours** is all about sharing the spotlight. Yes, you want to make sure you get your solo time in, stretching out on multiple choruses so you can play your heart out. But trading fours offers a unique challenge to the player and a treat to the audience, and can pay off for both.

Trading on 8-Bar Blues

Let's say you're playing with a trumpet player on a jazzy blues in B♭. You've played the head to your favorite blues tune, and each of you has played a solo. Instead of returning to the melody and closing out the song, you can trade some fours – four-bar phrases – and have some fun.

If you're playing an 8-bar blues, one of you will start with bars 1–4 and the other will follow with bars 5–8. Since you're playing piano, you will switch roles, from soloist to accompanist, accordingly. Here is what this might look like.

EXAMPLE 1

TRACK 39
0:00
CD 1

Bars 1–4 show a bluesy riff that gets a bit of variation treatment, much as you'd do when you solo. Bars 5–8 show more of a comping role, something you might play as you back up your friend on trumpet.

There won't be a chart with solo and comping parts written out, of course, when you do this. Example 2 shows what a typical chord chart might look like for an 8-bar blues, with the indications for solos added.

EXAMPLE 2

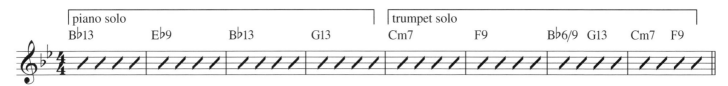

Trading on 12-Bar Blues

Now let's say you're playing with a guitar player, laying down some slow blues in G. If you start trading at bar 1 and solo through bar 4, the guitar will solo over bars 5–8, then you'll come back to solo some more over bars 9–12. Being the fair person you are, you'll make sure to trade for two choruses so you both get 12 bars of soloing in.

Here's what the first chorus might look like.

EXAMPLE 3

Math for Musicians

Keep in mind that you can trade phrases of other lengths in addition to four-bar phrases. If you're playing an 8-bar blues you can trade eigths (trade choruses) or trade twos. If you're playing 12-bar blues you can also trade 12s (trade choruses) or twos. If you trade with two other people, trading fours on a 12-bar blues works especially well since you'll play a chorus of blues each time you trade a round of solos (four bars each for three people = 12 bars).

LESSON #40: COMPING

Comping is the term used to describe what a pianist does while accompanying a singer, an instrumentalist, or a band. Simply stated, comping means playing the chord progression of a song. In general, there are three main functions of comping: 1) to provide a harmonic support to the song being played; 2) to give the chords a rhythmic context appropriate for the song; 3) to create space for the main element in any given situation (the melody, lead line, or solo). To do this a pianist has to have complete command of the chords in a song, be able to voice them in different ways, and play them rhythmically in different ways, all depending upon the style and context of the song.

Comping for a Traditional Blues

Example 1 shows some comping the first four bars of a traditional blues in C. Notice how the top notes in the right-hand part have a bit of melodic movement to them. Not too much, because it's important to stay out of the way of the melody or lead line. Also, the chords are all voiced in the mid-to-low register. This might be an appropriate way to comp when the melody or lead line is in a higher register and the tempo is not too fast.

EXAMPLE 1

You can see that this comping example leaves plenty of room for the melody or whatever might be the focal point of the music. There is some variation in the rhythms, so that it doesn't become too predictable, and very little in the way of fills that might be intrusive.

Now let's skip over to the last four bars of the same blues. Example 2 begins on the V chord in bar 9. Since there is a turnaround in bars 11 and 12, the comping here helps outline the fast-moving harmony of the turnaround, yet it isn't so busy that it would get in the way someone singing or soloing over the chords.

EXAMPLE 2

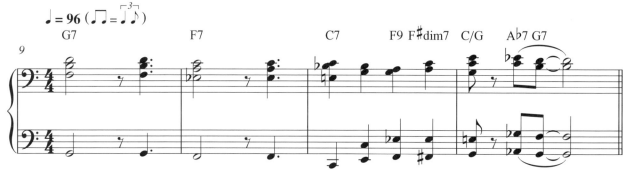

The previous examples use mostly four-note chords. It's a good idea to avoid too much doubling, and to avoid playing thick chords. You want to establish the harmony while keeping the texture as transparent as possible so other instruments can be heard.

Comping for a Jazz-Style Blues

Now let's take a look at some comping examples in a jazzy blues. Example 3 shows bars 1–4 of a blues in C. In contrast to Example 1, the voicings are quite a bit higher on the keyboard. Here the voicings use five or six notes, but there is still no doubling. Chords like these – with extensions like 9ths, 11ths, and 13ths – sound good played in a jazz setting.

EXAMPLE 3

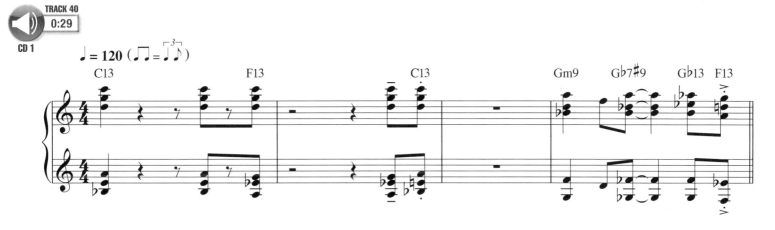

Focusing in on the rhythm, the chords play light syncopations in order to keep the beat swinging, leaving plenty of room open for a soloist.

Example 4 shows bars 9–12 of this same blues in C. Here the comping shows some typical techniques in jazz harmony: chromatic passing chords (Gb13 in between the G13 and F13), quartal voicings (chords built in 4ths), and a turnaround with lots of chord substitutions in bars 11 and 12.

EXAMPLE 4

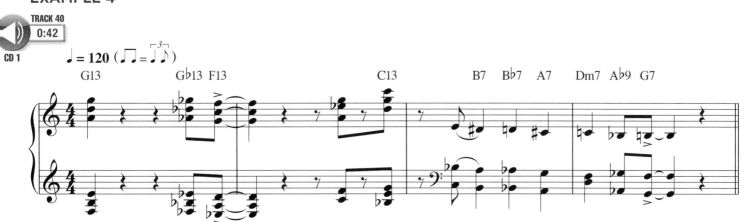

Comping Tips to Keep in Mind

- Lay down the chord progression.

- Give chords an appropriate rhythmic context.

- Create space for the melody or lead line.

LESSON #41: FILLS

In the right circumstances, you can be playing a blues for a good long while, repeating the 12- or 8-bar choruses quite a number of times. This gives you plenty of opportunity for adding **fills**. Finding a good place for fills always means listening to what's going on around you, whether it's a melody being sung or a solo being played. The right time could be a fill into the opening bar of the blues, leading into a chord change, a transition between choruses, or an ending that provides an opening for you and only you to fill. In this lesson we'll take a look at some of these opportunities and a few of the ways you can seize them.

Pickup Fills

Let's start with a quick pickup fill, using an E♭ pentatonic riff to jump into a blues in E♭. The triplet on beat 4 of Fill 1 is just enough to set up the tempo and feel, with the F♯ that leads into the triplet acting as a kind of step off the diving board. Fill 2 is a variation, with an added V chord in the left hand for harmonic support.

FILLS 1-2

For a more extended down-home style fill, Fills 3 and 4 take up a complete measure of 12/8 time and set up a slower blues in C. These fills have some tried-and-true piano licks built in, with plenty of notes from the C blues scale setting up the feel. The 3rds help give it a bit of a gospel feel, and the articulations give the 12/8 time signature a strong rhythmic reinforcement.

FILLS 3-4

Fills Between Phrases

Let's say you're comping along to a blues tune in F, and you feel a fill coming on as you go into the IV chord in bar 5. Fill 5 shows a triplet fill that quickly sets up the chord change while also adding a melodic element that fills beats 3 and 4 of bar 4.

FILL 5

Move on down to the last four bars of this same blues in F, and we'll add some tasteful fills to smooth the chord changes going from V to IV to I. Here, a simple chromatic fill leads into each chord change. Going into the V chord is a three-note fill leading chromatically from F to F# to G, which is the 5th of the chord, C9. Reverse the three-note fill and it leads down from the V chord to the IV chord, Bb9. And then going into bar 11, the same fill leads back to the I chord, F9, voiced with the 5th of the chord on top.

FILL 6

Ending Fills

The last two bars of a blues is the perfect place for showing off your most impressive fills. Fill 7 shows a long, descending fill for an F blues, using triplets and the F blues scale.

FILL 7

Taking things in a different direction, Fill 8 is an ascending fill into a big, fat ending chord – something you'd want for a grand finale. The right-hand fill spans two octaves as it climbs up the G pentatonic scale, with a few "blue" notes thrown in. In the left hand, octaves descend in contrary motion, creating a dramatic effect.

FILL 8

LESSON #42: CALL AND RESPONSE

Call and response is an effective device where a musical statement by one person or group is followed by a musical response by another person or group. Historically, it reaches back to spirituals and field hollers that have African cultural roots. A common example of musical call and response can be found in a religious ceremony between a preacher and congregation. Melodies of all types often have call-and-response patterns built into their structure, when their phrases have a question-and-answer quality. In this lesson we'll see how you can incorporate call-and-response patterns and concepts into your solo playing, and apply them to playing the blues.

One-Bar Patterns

The first way to incorporate call and response patterns is by trying out some one-bar phrases that follow the question-answer format. Riff 1 shows two short phrases in bars 1 and 3, followed by a response in bars 2 and 4.

RIFF 1

These examples have a symmetrical, matching quality to them. Each call and response has six notes. Although the rhythm of the responses is not identical to the rhythm of the calls, it is similar, and the responses give the feeling of completion, of answering the question posed by the call.

Now let's look at how an unmatched response can work to answer the call. The next riff shows a different approach to call and response.

RIFF 2

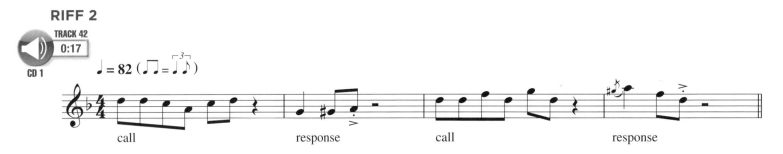

Two-Bar Patterns

Now let's apply this concept to two-bar phrases. The call in Riff 3 starts off the beat, with momentum that carries it into bar 2. The response is rhythmically similar, but takes the line to a higher peak before ending with a more emphatic descending line

RIFF 3

Alternating Registers

The benefits of playing the piano are many, and one of the most important is the ability to change registers quickly and easily. You can use register changes to highlight the call-and-response pattern, framing each within their own territory. Riff 4 shows one way you can do this.

RIFF 4

Now here's an opposite approach, starting with calls in the higher register and answering them with responses down lower on the keyboard.

RIFF 5

Alternating Textures and Dynamics

You can also play around with textures and dynamics as a way of contrasting and highlighting the call-and-response style. Riff 6, bars 1–4 of a blues in Eb, shows both hands working to achieve the same effect. The call is a simple, two-bar single-note statement in the right hand, played softly, with a walking bass in the lower register as its accompaniment. For the response, octave chords in the right hand paired with biting three-note chords in the left work together rhythmically for maximum punch and a big wall of sound.

RIFF 6

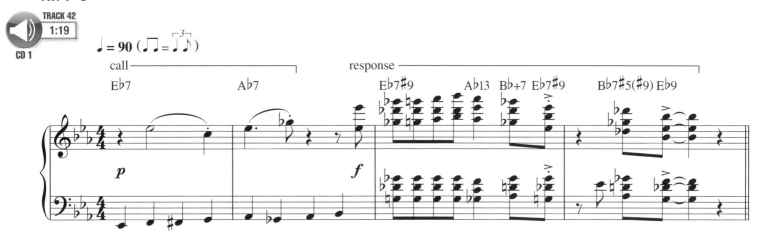

See how much you can do with call and response when you play. Eight- and 12-bar blues are perfect forms to experiment with all the different possibilities.

When you're thinking about solos, melodies, and riffs when you play the blues, you are quickly confronted with the question of what scales to use, and what sounds best when you're playing the three dominant 7th chords most commonly used, the I, IV, and V chords. **Major pentatonic scales** are a good place to start. With five notes, three of which are already in the chord, pentatonic scales can be effective as well as easy to master.

Blues in G

Say you're playing a blues in G. The I chord is a G7, and you can play a G major pentatonic scale for your melodic material. The pentatonic scale is made of the root, 2nd, 3rd, 5th, and 6th notes of the major scale.

You can use the notes in this scale any time you play the I chord. You can use the notes of a C pentatonic scale when you play the IV chord, C7. Riff 1 shows bars 1–4 of a 12-bar blues in G, using the G and C pentatonic scales for melodic material in this way.

RIFF 1

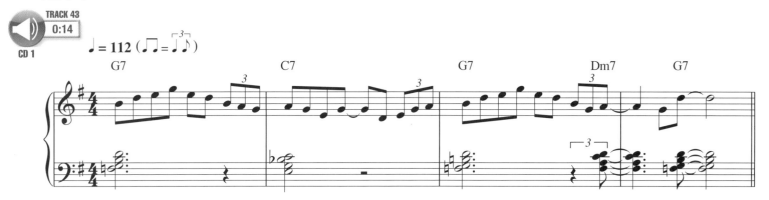

Note that the C and G pentatonic scales have four notes in common. Riff 2 shows bars 5–9 of a G blues, using the C pentatonic for bars 5 and 6 and the G pentatonic for bars 7 and 8.

RIFF 2

When you move to the V chord in bar 9, you can use the D pentatonic scale over the D7, and continuing on, use the C and G pentatonic scales for the IV and I chords, as follows:

RIFF 3

Adding Grace Note Slides

As you play these pentatonics you may feel they don't convincingly capture the blues style. You're right, because the blues style requires some grace note slides and such to give it a more authentic feel. Riff 5 shows how adding some slides really helps capture the style.

RIFF 4

Blues in B♭

Now let's look at some other pentatonic scales for other keys. In B♭, you can use the B♭ major pentatonic scale for the I chord and the E♭ pentatonic scale for the IV in bars 1–4 of a 12-bar blues. Riff 5 shows how effective pentatonic scales can be at a quicker tempo.

RIFF 5

Pentatonic scales are relatively easy to learn, and like the blues overall, ripe for all kinds of variation and experimentation. As you learn a new blues in a new key, start out by playing the pentatonic scales for the I, IV, and V chords, and gain fluency with each. Your riffs and melodies will take on new possibilities.

LESSON #44: MINOR PENTATONIC SCALES

Just as every major scale has a relative minor, a major pentatonic scale has a relative **minor pentatonic scale**. This is a very simple relationship: The 5th note of the major pentatonic scale, a major 6th above the root, is the root note of the relative minor pentatonic scale.

E Minor Pentatonic

The E minor pentatonic scale has the same notes as a G major pentatonic scale, but starts on an E rather than a G, as show below.

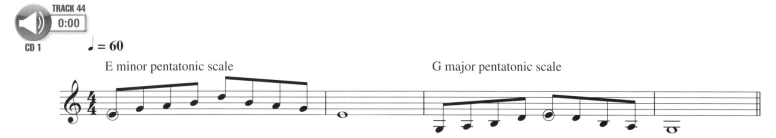

The interesting thing about using the minor pentatonic scale when you're playing the blues is that it automatically gives you the ♭7th and ♭3rd when played against a dominant chord. For example, in an E blues the I chord is an E7, with G♯ as the major 3rd. Playing an E minor pentatonic over the E7 will mean playing a D (the ♭7th) and a G♮ (the ♭3rd). Take a look at Riff 1 below to see this in action.

RIFF 1

The coolest thing about the minor pentatonic scale is that you can use it on all three chords of the blues – the I, IV, and V.

RIFF 2

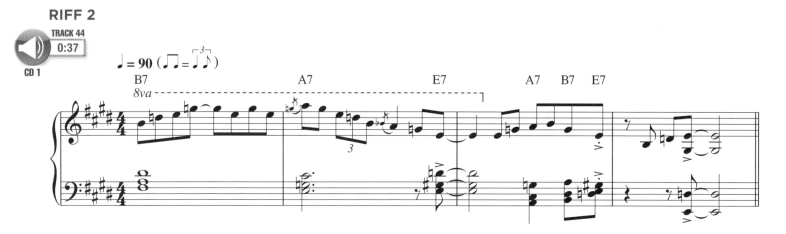

In this case, some notes of the E minor pentatonic are dissonant with notes in each of the three blues chords, but melodic use of the scale will usually override the dissonance. This highlights an important lesson for pianists playing the blues: The horizontal component (the melodic line) can function independently from the vertical component (the chord).

G Minor Pentatonic

Now let's take a look at the G minor pentatonic, which has the same notes as the B♭ major pentatonic. Here are bars 1–4 of a blues in G, using the G minor pentatonic for a riff.

RIFF 3

TRACK 44 0:53 CD 1

In the example above, the left-hand chords move through a traditional blues pattern based on the I chord G7. The right-hand line is independent, carrying out a melodic riff using the G minor pentatonic.

Here are more riffs using the G minor pentatonic, over bars 5–8 of a G blues (Riff 4) and 9–12 of a G blues (Riff 5).

RIFF 4

TRACK 44 1:10 CD 1

RIFF 5

TRACK 44 1:21 CD 1

LESSON #45: BLUES SCALES OVER DOMINANT 7TH CHORDS

In this lesson, we'll take a look at the notes that make up a **blues scale**, and explore how they can be used playing over dominant 7th chords in the blues. Blues scales build on pentatonic scales, so it helps to have a firm command of pentatonic scales as you learn the blues scales.

Blues Scale Anatomy

Example 1 shows the G blues scale. You'll see that the six notes in the scale add one note to the G minor pentatonic scale, the C♯ (or D♭).

EXAMPLE 1

Example 2 shows blues scales for C and F, two other common blues keys.

EXAMPLE 2

You can build a blues scale for any key: Start with the root, add the ♭3rd, 4th, ♭5th (or augmented 4th), and ♭7th.

Blues scales are unique for two reasons: They include the three "blue" notes (the ♭3rd, ♭5th, and ♭7th) and one blues scale can be used for melodies and riffs over all three chords in a traditional blues (the I, IV, and V).

Blues Scale Riffs

Riff 1 shows a two-bar riff based on a descending blues scale first in G, then transposed to C and to F.

RIFF 1

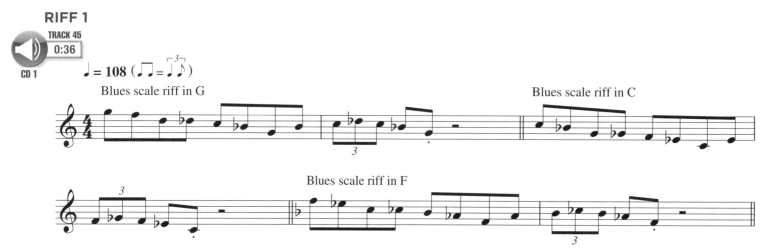

Tip: As you start learning blues riffs, it's good practice to run them through a few different keys this way, transposing them as you go so they become part of your riff repertoire.

Riff 2 shows an ascending blues riff in G over the first four bars of a G blues. The left-hand accompaniment is a simple syncopated chord pattern.

RIFF 2

TRACK 45
0:53
CD 1

Now try a different approach for a blues scale, this time in C. This riff alternates from the root note up to the other scale tones in a triplet rhythm. This works well in a slower blues with a railroad-style pattern in the left hand.

RIFF 3

TRACK 45
1:06
CD 1

For a blues in F, try a swing-style setting for the last four-bars of a 12-bar blues. This approach shows that you can take a portion of the scale and cycle it, creating an effective riff.

RIFF 4

TRACK 45
1:23
CD 1

The six-note blues scale is a lot of fun to work with. See how creative you can be in coming up with some of your own riffs by varying the patterns, rhythms and registers, and try them out over the blues chords.

BLUES SCALES OVER MINOR CHORDS

Blues scales are a natural fit when played over minor chords, because both share the ♭3rd as part of their makeup. Minor 7th chords also share the ♭7th with the blues scale. When playing a minor-key blues, blues scales are an excellent choice for melodies, riffs, and solos.

D Minor Blues

Let's start with D minor as our home key. Here is the D blues scale:

The D blues scale sounds good in almost any combination over a D minor triad, as Riff 1 shows.

RIFF 1

The same scale sounds good over the iv chord of a D minor blues, in this case a G minor.

RIFF 2

And when you add 7ths to the i and iv chords, you enhance the sound of the chords in combination with the blues scale.

RIFF 3

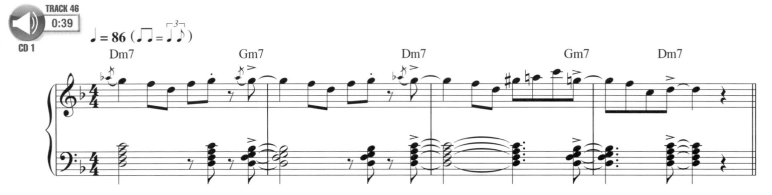

F Minor Blues

F minor is another favorite minor-key blues, and on piano, the F blues scale fits nicely under the fingers.

RIFF 4

The last four bars of a minor blues often use a ii-V-i progression. In F minor, this means a Gm7♭5 in bar 9, a C7 in bar 10, and an Fm7 in bars 11–12, often with a turnaround or end cadence. Riff 5 shows how nicely an F blues riff can sound over this progression.

RIFF 5

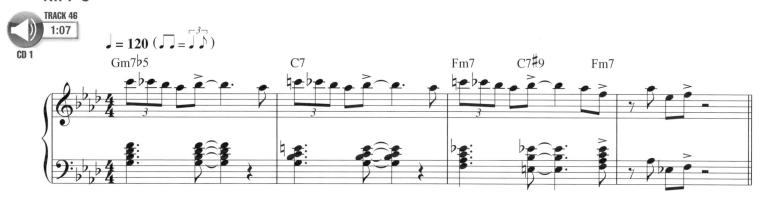

C Minor Blues

Riff 6 shows how much mileage you can get out of a blues scale, this time over the last eight bars of a C minor blues. Notice the different ways the blues scale can be used: A simple descending line in bar 5 with a short climb up over the iv chord in bar 6; a repeat with a variation in bar 8 over the i chord; a down-up pattern of upper chord notes to the root and back up in bars 9 and 10; as a grace note slide leading into bar 11; and in a punctuated ending for bar 12.

RIFF 6

The **Mixolydian scale** is a seven-note scale, like the major scale, and has all the same notes as a major scale except the 7th, which is flatted (lowered a half step). Along with the blues scale, it is a go-to scale to play over a dominant 7th chord because it has all four chord notes in the scale, and the remaining three notes function easily as passing notes between the chord notes.

The C Mixolydian Scale

The example below shows a C Mixolydian scale.

The seventh, B♭, is a half step lower than it would be if this were the C major scale. You can see that this scale has all the notes of an F major scale, but played from C to C rather than F to F. Its function in the blues is similar to its function as one of the Greek modes, with the C root and ♭7th giving it a sound unlike the major scale, more ambiguous and less resolved.

There are plenty of signature riffs and patterns in the blues that are built on the Mixolydian scale. Here are a couple familiar ones: the first a right-hand riff, and second, a left-hand pattern.

RIFFS 1-2

The Mixolydian scale can easily be applied to the blues by playing riffs based on the scale for each of the three blues chords: the I, IV, and V. Here are the last four bars of a 12-bar blues in C, with a G Mixolydian scale for the V chord, an F Mixolydian scale over the IV chord, and the C Mixolydian scale over the I chord.

RIFF 3

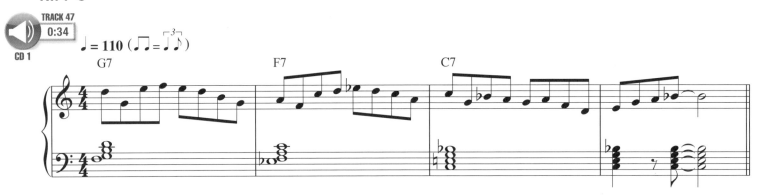

Of course, you don't have to try to play every scale note in every riff, so as you get comfortable with the scales you can be more selective with the scale notes.

RIFF 4

TRACK 47
0:48
CD 1

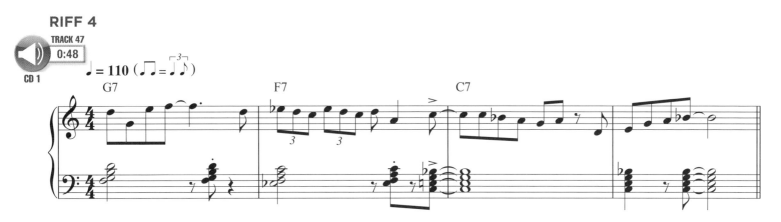

As you can hear, the 7th of each scale is really the choice note, because it represents the "blue" note – the ♭7th – and is the note that really captures the blues feel. Now let's take a look at some more mixolydian scales and riffs.

Mixolydian Possibilities

Here's a riff featuring the D Mixolydian scale in a stop-time section of a blues in D.

RIFF 5

TRACK 47
1:00
CD 1

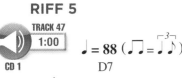

In an up-tempo swing blues, the Mixolydian scale lets you play long lines, exploring the ins and outs of the scale. Here are four bars from an F blues, with an F Mixolydian over the I chord (F7) and a B♭ Mixolydian over the IV chord (B♭7).

RIFF 6

TRACK 47
1:16
CD 1

Dressing up the Mixolydian with some bluesy ornaments really increases the possibilities. Riff 7 shows the last four bars of a blues in G, using a D Mixolydian over the D7, C Mixolydian over the C7, and a G Mixolydian over the G7. The feel here is a slow, down-home blues in 12/8. The left-hand part gets in on the Mixolydian action, too, with a pattern taken from each Mixolydian scale.

RIFF 7

TRACK 47
1:27
CD 1

LESSON #48: PLAYING ON THE BEAT

Starting Riffs on the Beats

Playing on the beat means starting or ending riffs on beats 1, 2, 3, or 4, or emphasizing these beats in your playing. Let's first take a look at starting your riffs on the beats. A good way to expand your options and flexibility as a player is to take a riff and move the starting point to another place, rhythmically speaking. So, for example you can begin with a riff that starts on beat 1, and then play the riff starting on beats 2, then 3, then 4. What you find is that it will open up possibilities you wouldn't hit upon in your normal practice.

Riff 1 shows how you follow through with this rhythmic exercise. It's a two-bar riff in B♭ that starts on beat 1 and moves to start on each remaining beat in sequence. Sometimes you'll want to adapt the rhythm of the riff to follow your instinct, as happens with this one. But the point is to keep the exercise on track by starting the riff on each of the four beats in the measure.

RIFF 1

Riff 2 takes a chordal riff that starts on beat 1 of a blues in G and moves it to start on the other beats in the measure. This riff is very beat-oriented, designed to emphasize every other beat. See what happens when it's moved to start on beats 2, 3, and 4.

RIFF 2

Ending Riffs on the Beats

Next let's take a riff and focus on placing the last note on the beats, moving it so it lands on the other beats as well. The goal is to allow yourself some creative license and still follow the exercise through to completion. Here, rather than move the starting point later in the measure, I kept it on beat 2 and moved the end point later each time.

RIFF 3

Playing Beat-Oriented Rhythms

You can also choose a beat in each measure for emphasis. Riff 4 is oriented around beat 3, and sets up a pattern of expectation that is met by the accented chord on beat 3 of bar 4.

RIFF 4

For a passage where you want to really drive home the beat, you can play a riff that really digs into each beat, like this beat-oriented passage. The eighth notes are not syncopated, but push to land on the next beat, and the chords on beat 4 develop a pattern that builds expectation with each bar.

RIFF 5

LESSON #49: PLAYING OFF THE BEAT

Moving It Off the Beat

This lesson shows you how you can build more syncopation into your playing, and open up your blues to a greater variety of rhythms to apply to your solos, riffs, and patterns. The first step is to take a simple idea with quarter notes that are on the beat, and move them forward to the "and" of 1, and back to the "and" of 4. Here's an example of how to move a riff off the beat.

RIFF 1

TRACK 49
0:00
CD 1

Next, take a riff that starts and stops on the beats, and move it forward and back to the offbeats. Notice how doing this encourages you to accent the offbeats, to really own the syncopations you're choosing.

RIFF 2

TRACK 49
0:24
CD 1

Now let's focus on a riff that ends on beat 1. Moving it off the beat affects the rhythmic structure of the riff, and compels you to change your left-hand accompaniment to maximize the syncopated results. Riff 3 shows a riff with four "on the beat" quarter notes and three "off the beat" variations. Moving a riff off the beat is a simple technique that yields a bounty of new ideas.

RIFF 3

TRACK 49
0:34
CD 1

Playing the Blues Using Rhythmic Displacement

You can experiment and explore moving rhythms off the beat while you play the blues. One way to do this is to take a one-bar riff that is beat oriented and play with offbeat variations as you develop the riff over the first four bars of a blues. Riff 4 shows this approach in a slow blues in G with a traditional blues pattern in the left hand. The rhythmic variation that occurs in bars 2, 3, and 4 shows one of the ways you develop a riff to create a longer phrase.

RIFF 4

Let's take a different one-bar riff in the same blues context for another example.

RIFF 5

And finally, let's see how this approach might play out over the last four bars of the same blues in G.

RIFF 6

Getting creative with rhythmic displacement requires you to set limitations on your playing in order to carry it out. But if you keep in mind that your goal is to move a riff off the beat while keeping the notes of the riff the same, you'll find you've opened a door to greater creative freedom.

LESSON #50: TRIPLET SWING

Swing Eighths

Swing eighths are eighth notes that are played with the feel of a triplet subdivision. If you take two consecutive eighth notes where the first is played on a beat, the second eighth is played as if it were the third note of a triplet subdivision of the beat. Example 1 illustrates this.

EXAMPLE 1

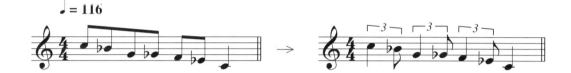

When blues, swing, and boogie were first published, these rhythms were often rendered as dotted eighths plus 16ths. You will frequently find older sheet music that looks like Example 2, below. Listen to the track to see how this sounds if you played the way it's written.

EXAMPLE 2

Since this results in a stilted, jerky feel, you have to adjust the rhythm as you play to make it swing with a triplet subdivision of the beats. Over the last 30 to 40 years, published music has corrected this by using a swing-eighth indicator above the time signature to indicate swing-eighth notes. This handy graphic can be found in most of these blues lessons. You'll now find the passage above written like this:

EXAMPLE 3

As you can see, this is a much easier way to read, and allows the player to imagine and render the eighth notes as swing eighths. Different blues styles have different ways of working with triplet swing, depending on how much or little emphasis and weight is given to the triplet subdivision. For example, in a slower, traditional blues, all three of the triplet rhythms can be emphasized, underlining the triplet feel by making it heard and felt through notes and rests, as in Riff 1.

RIFF 1

TRACK 50 0:28 CD 1

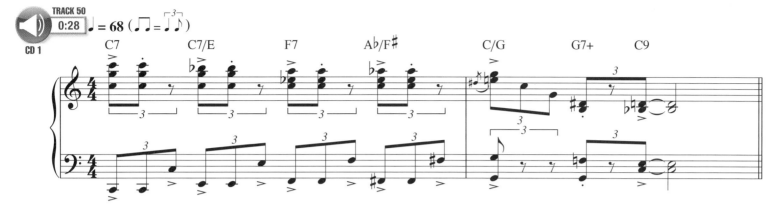

A country swing has a gentler triplet swing, getting a more relaxed feel by taking the emphasis off the second of the three notes in a triplet rhythm.

RIFF 2

TRACK 50 0:40 CD 1

A boogie shuffle might get its groove with heavy accents on the offbeat eighths and a rolling left-hand pattern. This feel has a strong downbeat on the first note of each triplet rhythm, and an accented upbeat that falls on the third note of each triplet rhythm.

RIFF 3

TRACK 50 0:56 CD 1

In a jazz context, triplet swing might be less overt, hinted at and felt underneath, but not as emphatically as in some other styles. Playing the first four bars of a jazzy blues, the rhythms might feature offbeat punctuation, lightly played, more open space, and more syncopation in general.

RIFF 4

TRACK 50 1:04 CD 1

As you play the blues, think about the rhythmic subtext: How are the beats divided, and how much or how little do you want to emphasize the beats and their divisions? The rhythmic choices you have are as limitless as they are exciting.

LESSON #51: THE COMPOSITE BLUES SCALE

The **composite blues scale** is the subject of this lesson. It is perhaps the most useful scale for playing solos and fills in blues keyboard. The composite blues scale is a combination of the notes in the major pentatonic scale and the notes of the minor blues scale.

The formula for the major pentatonic scale is: 1, 2, 3, 5, and 6.

EXAMPLE 1

The formula for the minor blues scale is: 1, ♭3, 4, ♭5, 5, and ♭7.

EXAMPLE 2

The composite blues scale results from combining these two scales. The formula for the composite blues scale is: 1, 2, ♭3, 3, 4, ♭5, 5, 6, and ♭7. The composite blues scale is a nine-note scale. It includes all the so-called blue notes: ♭3, ♭5, and ♭7.

EXAMPLE 3

The composite blues scale in C works great when playing solos or fills over the three chords in a standard 12-bar blues in C: C7, F7, and G7. You should avoid playing the natural 3rd (E♮) over the F7 chord, because it clashes with the E♭ in F7.

The composite blues scale in C does not sound right when playing a C minor blues because the natural 3rd (E♮) clashes with the E♭ in a C minor chord. Be aware of the fact that the composite blues scale works best for playing a standard 12-bar blues, with its dominant 7th chords over the first, fourth, and fifth degrees of the scale.

Following is a two-bar lick using the composite blues scale over a C7 chord.

EXAMPLE 4

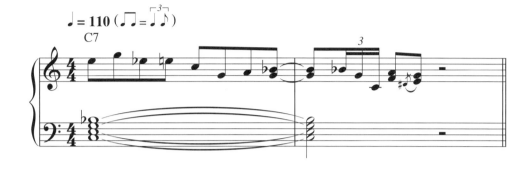

Here's another lick using the composite blues scale.

EXAMPLE 5

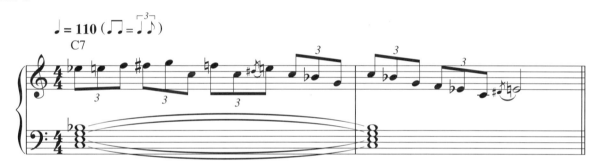

Finally, one more lick using the composite blues scale over a C7 chord.

EXAMPLE 6

Learn and practice the composite blues scale in every key. It will serve you well.

LESSON #52: SLOW BLUES IN 12/8

A **slow blues** is typically played in 12/8 meter. In this lesson, we'll look at blues keyboard patterns in 12/8 time.

In slow blues, the 12/8 meter has 12 eighth notes per bar, with each bar being divided into four strong pulses with three eighth notes falling on each pulse. The most common pattern for the right hand is repeated dominant 7th chords on each of the 12 eighth notes. The example below represents the first two bars of a 12-bar blues pattern in C. The left hand here simply plays held chord roots. Play the right hand chords as semi-detached.

EXAMPLE 1

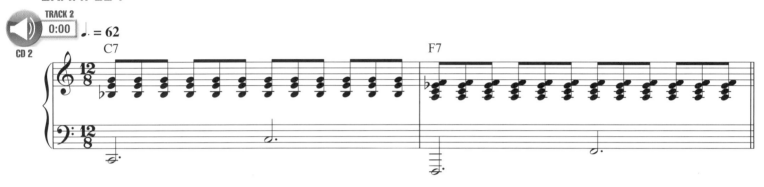

There is a standard left-hand pattern that is often used in slow blues. The pattern is built from broken chords (just the notes of the triad, omitting the 7th) in the following order: 1, 1 (an octave higher), 3, 5, 3 and 5. Here's that pattern used in the first two bars of a slow blues in C.

EXAMPLE 2

The left-hand pattern above is used not only blues, but in pop music as well. Fats Domino's "Blueberry Hill" prominently used this pattern. The song has a blues-like feel, but harmonically is not a 12-bar blues. The example below is in the style of the first four bars of "Blueberry Hill." The chords are generally played simply as triads, omitting the 7th.

EXAMPLE 3

A stride-like pattern is also commonly used in slow 12/8 blues. In **stride piano**, the left hand alternates between a bass note and a higher chord, as in Example 4. Note that the bass notes are the root and 5th or each chord. Also, note that the right hand is performing a **tremolo**, which is discussed in Lesson 53.

EXAMPLE 4

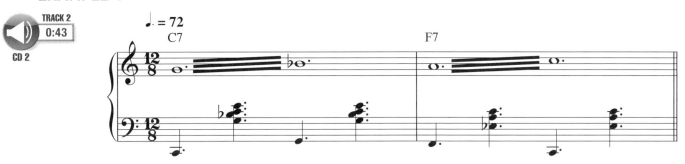

Another possibility in 12/8 slow blues is for the right hand to play eighth-note arpeggios with bass notes in the left hand. Each arpeggio spans approximately an octave, with the notes first going up and then coming back down.

EXAMPLE 5

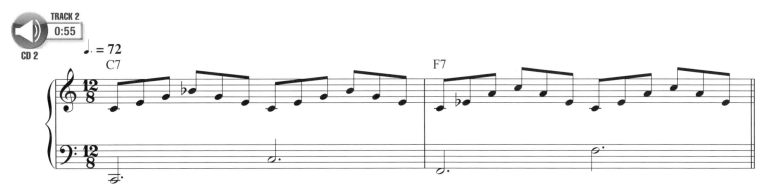

Learn these 12/8 patterns. They are very useful when playing slow blues.

LESSON #53: THE TREMOLO

The **tremolo** is a special keyboard technique used in blues and boogie-woogie. It is a rapid oscillation between two distinct notes or combinations of notes. On the keyboard, a quick rocking motion between the fingers of one hand produces the tremolo. Tremolos can consist of an octave, of smaller intervals (3rds and 6ths are common), or of full chords.

To play a tremolo, choose an interval larger than a whole step, such as a 3rd, and alternate playing the two notes as quickly as possible. The sheet music notation of a tremolo indicates that your fingers are "rolling" between the two notes. In fact, a tremolo is sometimes called a **roll**.

EXAMPLE 1

Tremolos occur frequently on 3rds, 6ths, or octaves.

EXAMPLE 2

Sometimes a tremolo consists of a whole chord.

EXAMPLE 3

Tremolos can be performed with both hands at once.

EXAMPLE 4

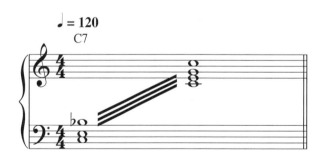

Tremolos are very effective with the ♭7th or the ♭3rd on the top of the interval.

EXAMPLE 5

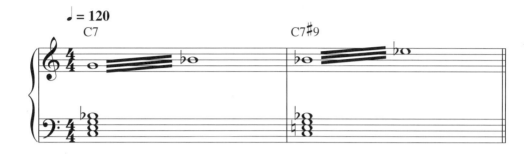

Tremolos can be combined with other ornamentations. Here is a classic figure: a tremolo between the 3rd and 5th of a major chord, embellished with a double grace note.

EXAMPLE 6

The next example is a short blues solo that uses the tremolo technique prominently. The left hand is playing a typical **barrelhouse pattern**.

EXAMPLE 7

Try using tremolos in your playing.

LESSON #54: THE GLISSANDO

A **glissando** (abbreviated as *gliss.*) is a slide or glide on the piano keys. A glissando can either ascend or descend. Descending glissandos are more common. Glissandos can use either the white keys or the black keys. White key glissandos are more common.

To perform a descending glissando, place the thumbnail of your right hand on a high note on the keyboard with your thumbnail facing to the left. Then drag your thumb down from right to left across the keys toward the lower keys.

To perform an ascending glissando, place the nail of your right middle finger on a low note with the nail facing right. Then drag your finger up from left to right across the keys toward the top of the keyboard.

When you perform a glissando, make sure that only your fingernails touch the keys, because it's easy to break your cuticle if you drag skin across the keys.

Example 1 shows how a glissando is notated: with a wavy line and the abbreviation *gliss.* The wavy line goes from the note you start on to approximately the note you end on.

EXAMPLE 1

Example 2 is an eight-bar solo, representing bars 5–12 of a 12-bar blues progression in G, that uses the glissando prominently. The left hand plays a walking bass. Note that all the glissandos are descending. Sometimes such glissandos are referred to as **fall-offs**. The glissandos here are performed in a specific syncopated rhythm.

EXAMPLE 2

When playing any blues or boogie-woogie, try incorporating glissandos. Jerry Lee Lewis virtually made a career out of it.

LESSON #55: BLUES INTROS – FAST BLUES

There are many ways to begin a quick 12-bar blues. A common way is to play the last four bars of the 12-bar blues progression and add a turnaround on the last two bars.

EXAMPLE 1

Another intro frequently played is based on I7, IV7, I7, and a lead-in to the V7 chord. This kind of intro often has a melodic lead-in to the first chord. In this example, it's the first four melodic notes.

EXAMPLE 2

The following is commonly referred to as the "Count Basie Blues Intro." It's just two bars.

EXAMPLE 3

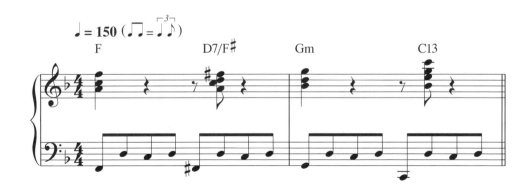

Another option for an intro is to start with the blues progression, with stops on beat one of each of the first four bars. The full rhythm then kicks in on bar 5, at the first change to IV7. Example 4 represents the first four bars of a blues in F, including a few melodic lead-in notes. The full rhythm would kick in at the next bar (not shown here) on the B♭7 (IV7) chord.

EXAMPLE 4

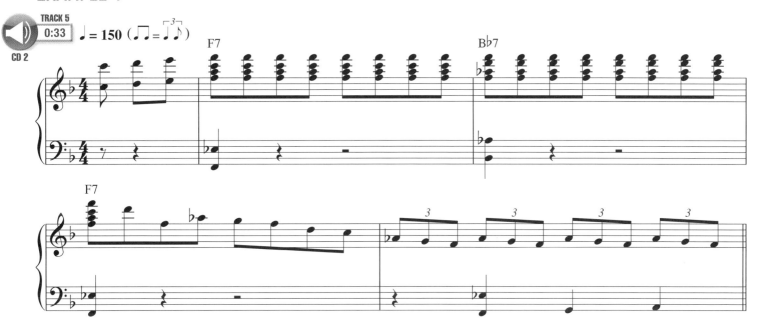

If you're playing a blues with a standard bass pattern, such as the barrelhouse pattern in the next example, or any of the boogie-woogie style left-hand patterns, you can begin by simply playing the boogie-woogie bass pattern for a few bars. The following example also includes a few chordal punches over the left-hand barrelhouse pattern. After vamping for a while (say, after four bars), everyone can join in and that becomes bar 1 of the 12-bar blues progression.

EXAMPLE 5

Learn various blues intros. All of them are useful and you never know what will be expected of you at a blues gig.

LESSON #56: BLUES INTROS – SLOW BLUES

A typical intro in 12/8 slow blues is to play the last four bars of the blues progression with a turnaround on the last two bars. The following example features repeated eighth-note triads in the right hand, the slow blues left-hand bass pattern and a standard turnaround in both hands.

EXAMPLE 1

TRACK 6
0:00
CD 2

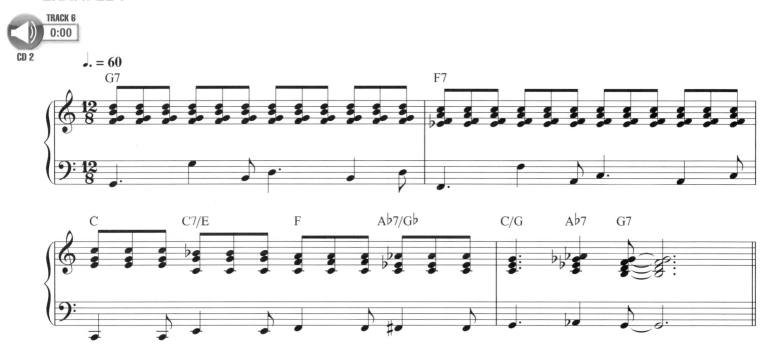

Sometimes the intro can be shortened to two bars.

EXAMPLE 2

TRACK 6
0:19
CD 2

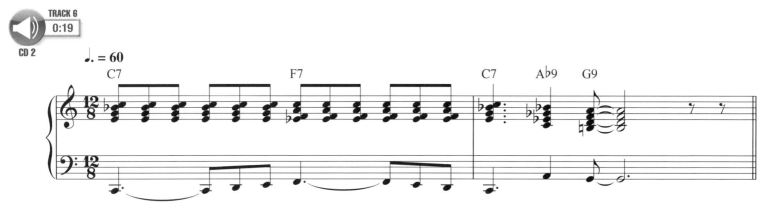

A stride pattern can be used in the left hand. Example 3, based on the last four bars of a standard blues progression, features a stride pattern in the left hand in bars 9 and 10, and blues licks in the right hand. It's followed by a standard turnaround.

EXAMPLE 3

Sometimes an intro to a slow blues can be as simple as an arpeggiated V7 chord. In the next example, the V7 chord at the beginning has a raised 5th. The blues then begins after one bar of the held chord.

EXAMPLE 4

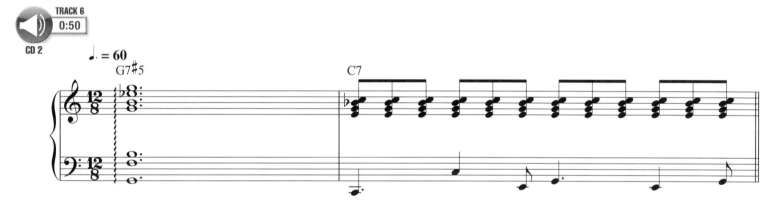

Another pattern sometimes used is the I-VI7-iim7-V7 progression. Example 5 alters both the IV7 chord and the V7 chord, and the I chord is played as a C6.

EXAMPLE 5

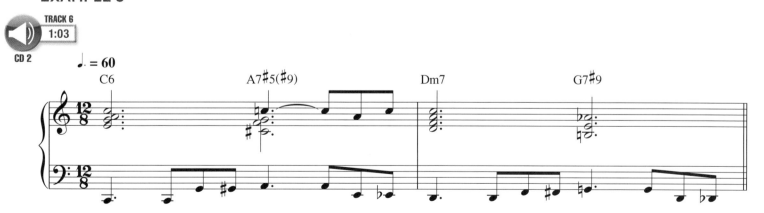

Familiarize yourself with these introductions.

LESSON #57: BLUES ENDINGS

The standard 12-bar blues both begins and ends on the I7 chord, so it may not always be clear where one chorus begins and the other ends. Therefore, bars 11 and 12 of the form often feature a turnaround, a chord progression that ends on V7 to lead us back to the beginning of the blues form.

Blues endings also occur over bars 11 and 12 of the form and are stylistically similar to turnarounds. However, blues endings generally end with a V7-I progression. A typical blues ending might include a bass walk-up that goes from I7 to V7 back up to I7, as in the following example.

EXAMPLE 1

TRACK 7
0:00
CD 2

A common alternative is a bass walk-down from I7 to V7 to I7.

EXAMPLE 2

TRACK 7
0:07
CD 2

These two ideas are often combined by putting the descending line in the right hand and the ascending line in the left. This results in a classic blues ending.

EXAMPLE 3

TRACK 7
0:14
CD 2

Another common ending is actually referred to as the **blues ending**. It includes a chromatic walk-down in the left hand with parallel 3rds in the right that alternate with a higher tonic note.

EXAMPLE 4

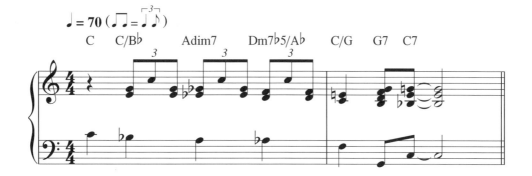

Here's a variation of the walk-down.

EXAMPLE 5

Finally, here's an ending favored by Willie Tee that has a New Orleans feel.

EXAMPLE 6

Learn these stylized endings in as many keys as possible.

LESSON #58: DOUBLE NOTES & DRONE NOTES

Playing **double notes** with one of the notes as a **drone note** is a technique commonly used in the right hand in blues keyboard. A drone note is a repeated note above or below a moving line or phrase. Example 1 shows a line using the C minor blues scale with the drone note of the tonic C on top.

EXAMPLE 1

Drone notes are commonly used in repeated triplet phrases:

EXAMPLE 2

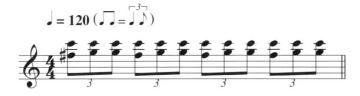

Example 3 uses drone notes on the bottom of the double notes

EXAMPLE 3

Grace notes are commonly used in drone notes phrases. Again, the drone note here is the tonic note C.

EXAMPLE 4

Example 5 shows a phrase that features a drone note on top:

EXAMPLE 5

The first four bars of a blues in C are given in Example 6. The left hand uses the barrelhouse pattern in eighth notes, while the right hand features double-note triplets in bars 1 and 2 and phrases with the drone note of C on top in bars 3 and 4.

EXAMPLE 6

TRACK 8
0:36
CD 2

Experiment with using double notes with a drone on top or bottom of the interval.

LESSON #59: PARALLEL 3RDS & PARALLEL 6THS

Keyboard blues are often built out of one- or two-bar licks in the right hand, which are repeated and varied throughout the blues form. Licks using **parallel 3rds** and **parallel 6ths** are particularly common. The 3rds or 6ths can move in either ascending or descending fashion. The 3rds or 6ths eventually resolve into the notes of the chord they are played over.

Example 1 is a lick from Clarence "Pinetop" Smith's "Pinetop's Boogie-Woogie." The descending parallel 3rds are combined with other notes interspersed between the 3rds in the right hand.

EXAMPLE 1

Next is a lick similar to something Jimmy Yancey would play.

EXAMPLE 2

Example 3 shows another common lick using parallel 3rds moving up and then downward.

EXAMPLE 3

Licks based on parallel 6ths also work well, such as the following:

EXAMPLE 4

Example 5 represents the first four bars of a blues in C. The first lick features ascending parallel 3rds. This lick is echoed in the next bar. The lick is then expanded on in bar 3 and in bar 4 the lick is played in descending fashion.

EXAMPLE 5

Experiment with parallel 3rds and 6ths. They are a common element in blues keyboard.

REPEATED NOTES, INTERVALS, & CHORDS

Another right-hand technique in keyboard blues is to use repeated notes, repeated octaves, repeated intervals, or repeated chords in the right hand. Repetition is a characteristic of blues in general. Such repeated patterns bring out the percussive nature of the piano.

Example 1 shows repeated notes in triplets.

EXAMPLE 1

Repeated intervals of a 3rd have a great blues sound.

EXAMPLE 2

Repeated octaves have a nice ringing sound on the piano.

EXAMPLE 3

Repeated chords are also common. The chords can be triads, 7ths, or other chords. They sound good whether you are comping or playing a solo.

EXAMPLE 4

Example 5 is based on the first four bars of a blues in C, with a standard left-hand pattern. Bars 1 and 2 feature repeated chords in triplet rhythms in the right hand. Bar 3 uses repeated intervals and bar 4 uses repeated octaves.

EXAMPLE 5

Repetition is a general characteristic of all blues music. Make good use of repeated notes, intervals, or chords.

USING TONE CLUSTERS & DISSONANCE

The blues keyboardist sometimes simultaneously strikes two or more notes situated a whole step or a half step apart. This is called a **tone cluster**. It adds excitement to the inherent drive of the blues.

The great boogie-woogie pianist Meade Lux Lewis had a particular fondness for tone clusters. At times, these created quite a dissonant sound. Example 1 is in the style of Meade Lux Lewis. There are six notes in the right-hand cluster. Thus, each finger must play one note, with the lowest two notes of the cluster both being played by the thumb.

EXAMPLE 1

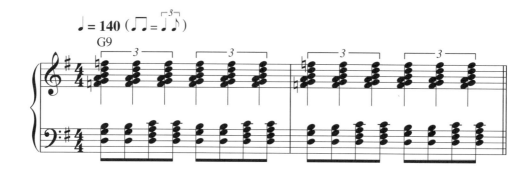

Often, as in the example above, the right hand cluster is played in a rhythm that contrasts with the underlying beat. The next example, also in the style of Lewis, features a walking octaves left hand. The cluster that falls on beat 2 of the first bar is particularly dissonant.

EXAMPLE 2

Example 3 also uses walking octaves in the left hand. The chord in the right hand includes both the major 3rd and the minor 3rd for an intentionally dissonant sound.

EXAMPLE 3

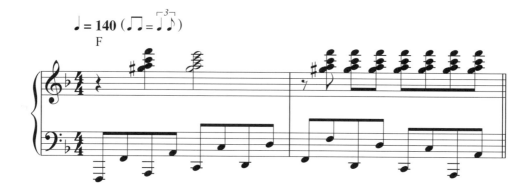

Count Basie is the model for the next example. The left-hand pattern is fairly standard. The cluster in bars 1–3 contains both the major and minor 3rd of the C chord. The cluster in bar 4 is in a rhythm that contrasts with the underlying beat.

EXAMPLE 4

Experiment with tone clusters and intentional dissonance. It can really spice up your playing.

Two-beat descending riffs are common in the right hand in keyboard blues. In a two-beat descending riff, the first half-beat is a single note, an interval, or a chord. The rest of the pattern forms a descending figure with the second half of the first beat made up of 16th notes, 16th-note triplets, or 32nd notes. The second beat consists of two eighth notes.

Sometimes the two-beat descending riff constitutes a major chord, as in Example 1.

EXAMPLE 1

Sometimes the two-beat descending riff may constitute a 6th chord.

EXAMPLE 2

Sometimes the two-beat descending riff outlines a dominant 7th chord.

EXAMPLE 3

The two-beat descending riff can even be made out of a cluster, such as the following, in which both the major 3rd and the minor 3rd of the chord are played together.

EXAMPLE 4

Next, let's put two-beat descending riffs to work in the first four bars of a blues in C, with a standard barrelhouse left hand.

EXAMPLE 5

Practice developing your own two-beat descending riffs.

LESSON #63: JUMP BLUES

The **jump blues** is a style that features up-tempo, happy, often humorous songs with a danceable shuffle rhythm. The greatest proponent of jump blues was bandleader Louis (pronounced "Louie") Jordan (1908–1975) and his band, the Tympany Five. The band had dozens of hits in the 1940s and 1950s. Jordan, who was a singer and sax player, wrote and recorded humorous songs such as "Caldonia," "Choo Choo Ch'Boogie," "There Ain't Nobody Here But Us Chickens," and "Is You Is or Is You Ain't (Ma Baby)." These songs have become blues standards.

Jump blues usually follows the standard 12-bar progression, although bars 9 and 10 are often turned into a bar of iim7 and a bar of V7. Also, the IV chord in bar 2 is often skipped in favor of the I chord played for the first four bars. Instead of using dominant 7th chords, the jump blues more often uses 6th chords for I and IV. Jump blues always uses a strong shuffle rhythm in a moderate to fast tempo. The bass typically walks throughout, outlining the notes of a 6th chord or a 7th chord. The right hand of the piano often plays chords in upbeats on every beat. The upbeats are played in a detached manner, while the left hand is played legato. Example 1 is a typical jump blues pattern over a C6 chord.

EXAMPLE 1

Example 2 is a variation of the pattern over a C7 chord.

EXAMPLE 2

Here are bars 9–12 of a typical jump blues, using the iim7 and V7 chords.

EXAMPLE 3

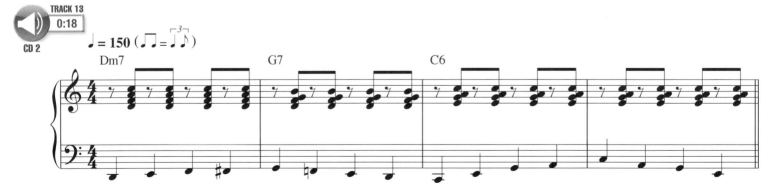

Jump blues songs often make use of repeated instrumental riffs. The riff mays be repeated exactly or the notes may be altered slightly to fit the chords, as in Example 4.

EXAMPLE 4

TRACK 13
0:28
CD 2

Jump blues sometimes uses stops, as in the chorus of "Caldonia." After two stops, the band bangs out the punch line in unison quarter-note triplets: "What makes your big head so hard?"

EXAMPLE 5

TRACK 13
0:44
CD 2

For a whole lotta fun, listen to jump blues.

LESSON #64: THE FAMOUS LICK

A **lick** is a short phrase that's used in melodies, solos or fills. An indispensable part of the keyboard blues vocabulary is the crossover, resolving right-hand lick. This lick is so prominent that Dr. John calls it **The Famous Lick**.

It's a crossover lick, because the descending phrase requires the fingers of the right hand to cross over the thumb on their way to the lower notes in the lick. The lick is also "resolving" in the fact that it ends with a half-step resolution into the 3rd of the chord it's built on.

Below are many variations of The Famous Lick. They are all in the key of C. These licks would work well over either the C or C7 chords. The lick is particularly effective when played in bar 11 of the 12-bar blues progression.

The first lick is the simple, classic crossover lick.

EXAMPLE 1

The next lick is in the style of Huey "Piano" Smith. Listen to the beginning of his R&B hit "Rockin' Pneumonia and the Boogie-Woogie Flu."

EXAMPLE 2

The next lick has a little Allen Toussaint in it. It uses some lead-in notes.

EXAMPLE 3

Fats Domino might play the lick something like this:

EXAMPLE 4

James Booker might play it like Example 5.

EXAMPLE 5

Here are a few more ways to play The Famous Lick:

EXAMPLE 6

EXAMPLE 7

EXAMPLE 8

How you play "The Famous Lick" is an important part of your style. Every blues keyboardist makes it individual.

The minor pentatonic scale (1, ♭3, 4, 5, ♭7) is often used to create blues licks. Example 1 is based on a descending C minor pentatonic scale.

EXAMPLE 1

The major pentatonic scale (1, 2, 3, 5, 6) also works well.

EXAMPLE 2

Repeated triplet patterns are common.

EXAMPLE 3

You can create interesting effects by playing a three-note pattern in a four-note rhythm, such as the three-note pattern (F♯, G, C) done in 4/4 time.

EXAMPLE 4

The three-note pattern (D♯, E, C) in Example 5 also works well in 4/4.

EXAMPLE 5

Here's a four-note pattern (D♯, E, G, G) done in triplets, creating an interesting rhythm.

EXAMPLE 6

Example 7 a five-note pattern (C, D♯, E, G, A) done in a triplet rhythm.

EXAMPLE 7

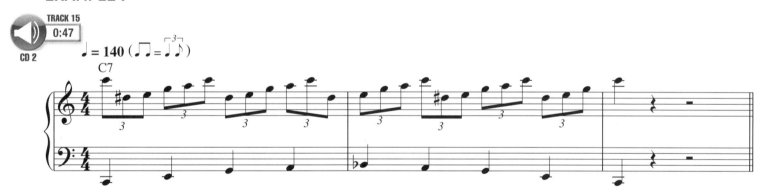

Another four-note pattern (B♭, A, G, E) done in a triplet rhythm is given below.

EXAMPLE 8

Experiment with patterns of notes done in different rhythms.

LESSON #66: BARRELHOUSE BLUES

Blues piano had its origins in the southern United States in the late 1800s and early 1900s in the rough-and-tumble barrelhouses in the railroad, mining, lumber, and turpentine camps. Barrelhouses were cheap drinking establishments where liquor was sold from wooden barrels. Most such establishments had a beat-up upright piano as the center of entertainment. Pianists drifted from camp to camp looking for places to play. The pianists adapted to the limitations of the pianos with ingenuity. They developed an aggressive style to be heard above the crowd. Barrelhouse players didn't tickle the ivories – they smashed them.

The **left-hand barrelhouse blues pattern** consists of an alternation between the intervals of a 5th and a 6th in the left hand. This is one of the most common left-hand patterns in blues. Pay attention to the fingering: Use fingers 2 and 5 for the interval of a 5th and 1 and 5 for the interval of a 6th. That way, you don't have to move your thumb.

EXAMPLE 1

The rhythms are often doubled into eighth notes. Barrelhouse usually uses swing eighths.

EXAMPLE 2

The barrelhouse style follows the 12-bar blues progression, often leaving out the IV chord in bar 2 and playing four bars of I instead. A typical comping rhythm might include chords in the right hand played in a syncopated rhythm, as in Example 3.

EXAMPLE 3

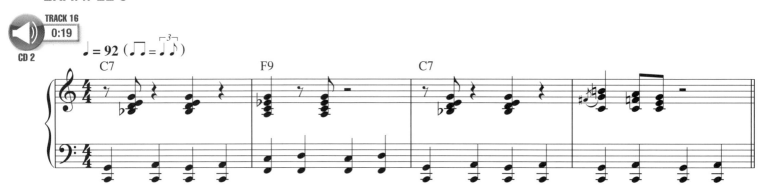

Barrelhouse blues frequently have melodic lead-ins, as in Example 4. Repeated triplet rhythms are often used in the right hand, as are figures based on parallel 3rds.

EXAMPLE 4

TRACK 16
0:33
CD 2

The left-hand barrelhouse pattern can be used in almost any style of blues. I consider the pattern to be a fallback that works in almost every situation: When you are in doubt, or when the rhythm starts to get wobbly, you can always fall back on the barrelhouse pattern.

LESSON #67: USING TRITONES

The **tritone** is an interval equal to the sum of three whole steps. It can be spelled as an augmented 4th or a diminished 5th. When playing the blues, the tritone can often be used in the place of a complete dominant 7th chord. Tritones work when played by either the right or left hand.

The tritone works great in the left hand when you are performing with a bass player. The bass will cover the roots of the chords, while the tritone creates a nice chord shape that sounds complete with the addition of the bass note.

Tritones in blues are made up of the 3rd and the 7th of the chords. The tritones can be played with either the 3rd or the 7th on the bottom. For example, If playing a blues in C, you could use the following tritones for the three chords: C7, F7, and G7 in the left hand.

EXAMPLE 1

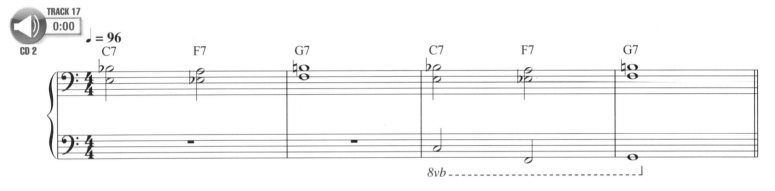

The first tritone has the 3rd on the bottom and the next two have the 7th on the bottom. However, you could also play the chords like this:

EXAMPLE 2

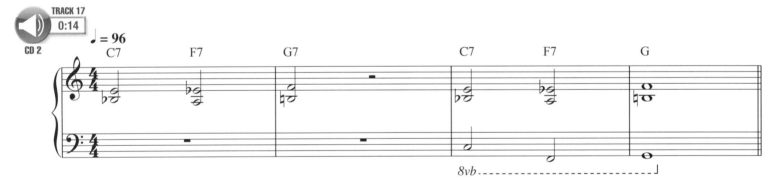

In Example 2, the C7 has the 7th on the bottom and the other two chords have the 3rd on the bottom. The idea is to use tritones that are close to each other on the keyboard, so that you have to move your hand as little as possible.

Here are the first four bars of a blues in F, using tritones in the left hand. We've given the tritones a characteristic rhythm. This sort of left hand works well only when you're performing with a bass player.

EXAMPLE 3

TRACK 17
0:28
CD 2

The tritone also sounds good on chords used in a typical turnaround in bars 11 and 12, as in Example 4. For the best results, don't play the tritones with any note of the interval lower than an octave below middle C. Otherwise, it could sound too muddy.

EXAMPLE 4

TRACK 17
0:45
CD 2

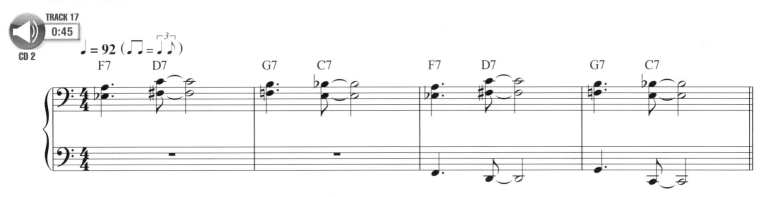

Tritones can also be played in the right hand, while the left hand plays a walking bass line. This would be in the event that you are not performing with a bass player.

EXAMPLE 5

TRACK 17
0:59
CD 2

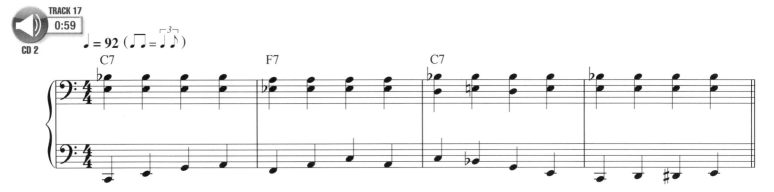

Learn to use tritones in either hand in place of dominant 7th chords.

LESSON #68: EXTENDING TRITONES INTO MORE COMPLEX VOICINGS

Tritones in the left hand can be extended with one note (or more than one note) to create richer sounds. Here are the tritones for the I7, IV7, and V7 chords in the key of C. (The tritones are then played with their corresponding bass notes.)

EXAMPLE 1

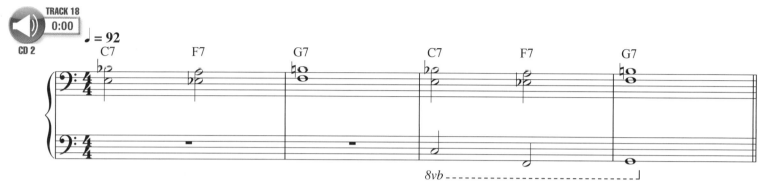

These tritone voicings can be enriched by adding another note to each chord. (A **voicing** is the vertical spacing and ordering of the pitches in a chord.) For example, you could add a 9th to the I7 chord and a 13th to both the IV7 and V7 chords. Then the chord voicings would become those shown in Example 2. (On the CD, the voicings are then played with their corresponding bass notes.)

EXAMPLE 2

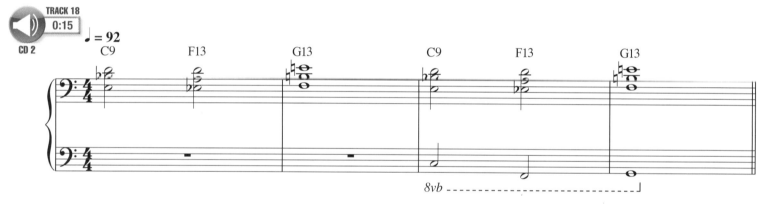

Such three-note rootless chord voicings are commonly used in jazz and they also work well in blues *when you are performing with a bass player*. If you are playing solo, you still want to play the chords in root position.

Example 3 uses two-note tritone voicings in the context of the first four bars of a C blues. The tritones are played twice in each bar using a syncopated rhythm. Also try using the three-note voicings in this same context.

EXAMPLE 3

The three-note left hand voicings can be further enriched by adding yet another note. Here are some voicings that add a note to each chord that is a second apart from one of the other notes in the chord. This gives the chords a stimulating, slightly dissonant sound.

EXAMPLE 4

These voicings can be opened up (spaced out) and split between the two hands.

EXAMPLE 5

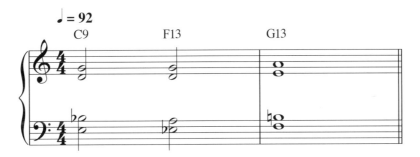

Example 6 is a typical rhythmic pattern for playing two-handed, five-note chords in the context of a C blues, when performing with a bass player.

EXAMPLE 6

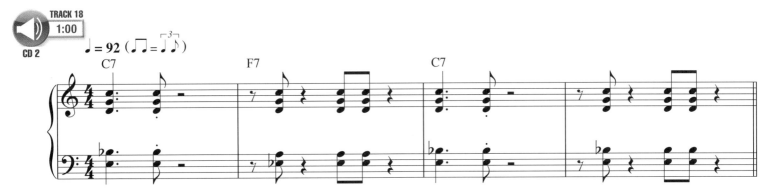

Finally, you can make the voicings even more harmonically complex. Space the chords between both hands and add another note that hasn't previously been used in the chord to make six-note voicings. Such chords are stacked using intervals of a tritone, a 4th, or a 3rd.

EXAMPLE 7

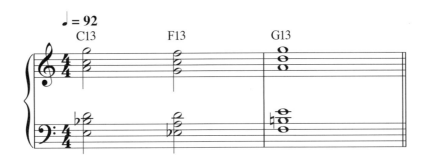

LESSON #69: FUNKY BLUES

Blues with a funky feel have been recorded by many blues artists. **Funk** emphasizes the rhythmic groove of the interlocking parts played by the electric guitar, bass, drums and keyboard parts. The groove in funk is almost always a straight-eighth groove. One of the keys to success when performing **funky blues** is not to overplay. Pare down your part so that it interlocks with the parts played by the other musicians.

Let's start with a funky keyboard voicing for the C7 chord, with an added E♭. That makes the chord a C7♯9. The chord is usually voiced as a stack from the lowest to highest notes: the major 3rd, the dominant 7th, and the ♭3rd. The 5th of a C7♯9 is generally not played. The root is played either by the bass player or by the left hand of the piano. Example 1 has the funky three-note voicing for both the right and left hands.

EXAMPLE 1

Example 2 is the first two bars of a typical funky blues groove. The chord progression usually follows the standard 12-bar blues pattern, but often leaves the IV chord out of the second bar. The IV7 and V7 chords are generally not played with a ♯9, only the I chord.

EXAMPLE 2

Here's a bit of a possible melody for our groove.

EXAMPLE 3

There's a standard James Brown horn lick that also works well on keys. The lick is based on intervals of a tritone in the right hand. It uses the 3rd of the chord on the bottom and the 7th on top, or the 7th on the bottom and the 3rd on top. The tritones move chromatically down one half step, then back up to where they began. Here are the licks over the C7 and F7 chords.

EXAMPLE 4

Example 5 demonstrates another funky blues groove, using the three-note shape for the C7♯9 chord in the right hand.

EXAMPLE 5

The next example uses a tritone in the right hand.

EXAMPLE 6

Finally, the chord shape for a C7♯9 chord is used in the left hand in another funky blues groove.

EXAMPLE 7

Familiarize yourself with some funky blues.

JERRY LEE LEWIS & EARLY ROCK 'N' ROLL

Jerry Lee Lewis (b. 1935) was – and is – a terrific boogie-woogie and blues pianist. He is one of the pioneers of rock 'n' roll, with hit songs such as "Great Balls of Fire" and "Whole Lotta Shakin' Goin On." Almost all the early rock 'n' roll songs were based on a 12-bar blues progression. (Sometimes it was an eight-bar blues.) Most used a boogie-woogie pattern in either the guitar or the left hand of the piano.

Lewis usually employed standard boogie-woogie patterns in his left hand, such as those in Example 1. He almost always played with straight eighths, a characteristic of rock 'n' roll, as opposed to the swing music that preceded it.

EXAMPLE 1

TRACK 20
0:00
CD 2

Lewis's right hand was characterized by repeated chords, usually dominant 7th chords, banged out in a propulsive eighth-note rhythm.

EXAMPLE 2

TRACK 20
0:16
CD 2

Sometimes Lewis would play a ♭3rd in the repeated I7 chords, giving the music a raucous quality.

EXAMPLE 3

TRACK 20
0:23
CD 2

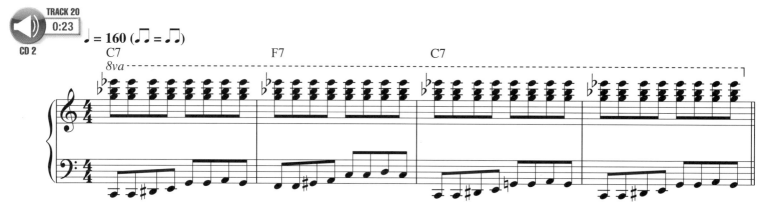

Example 4 demonstrates a typical comping pattern that Lewis used in his right hand, while he played a standard boogie/blues pattern in his left hand.

EXAMPLE 4

Lewis was fond of the two-beat descending riffs in his right hand.

EXAMPLE 5

He also used the **yodel lick** in his right hand. This lick is still heard in country piano. Lewis got it from his hero, Western Swing pianist Moon Mullican. Lewis also used the glissando, both ascending and descending varieties, glisses with both hands going different ways, etc. almost compulsively.

EXAMPLE 6

There are no lessons in this book covering some of Lewis's other techniques, such as stomping on the keys with his right leg or sitting on the keyboard. You'll have to figure those out for yourself.

LESSON #71: COUNT BASIE STYLE

William "Count" Basie (1904–1984) was an American jazz pianist, organist, composer, and band leader. In 1935 Basie formed his own jazz orchestra in Kansas City and led the group for 50 years.

Basie favored blues and was excellent at playing both boogie-woogie and stride styles. Basie's version of the blues progression came into wide use. It featured a ♯iv diminished chord in bar 6 following the IV chord in bar 5. He also generally used the V7 chord in both bars 9 and 10.

Basie often used walking octaves in his left hand. The octaves didn't always follow the usual chord outlines. Here's an example of what he sometimes played as a walking octaves bass on the I7 chord in bars 1–4 of a blues progression:

EXAMPLE 1

Example 2 shows two other left-hand patterns he frequently used.

EXAMPLE 2

In his right hand, Basie often used an open-spaced voicing of the dominant 7th chord in a punched rhythm:

EXAMPLE 3

He often used 6th chords, including chord outlines, as melodies. He was also fond of the repeated triplet lick.

EXAMPLE 4

Basie liked to use intentional dissonance. The repeated chord in the following example uses both the major 3rd and the minor 3rd of the chord.

EXAMPLE 5

TRACK 21
0:32
CD 2

One other device he often used was a piano break played in either octaves, or sometimes double octaves, over the I7 chord for four bars before the song went back to the blues progression starting in bar 5. Here's such a break:

EXAMPLE 6

TRACK 21
0:41
CD 2

Check out Count Basie's recordings. There's a reason he was called the "Count."

LESSON #72: FATS DOMINO STYLE

Antoine "Fats" Domino (born in 1928 in New Orleans) became one of the biggest rock 'n' roll stars of the 1950s. He had more hits between 1949 and 1962 than any other rocker besides Elvis Presley. Musicians such as Paul McCartney have acknowledged Domino as an influence.

Domino was an excellent boogie-woogie pianist and his popular music style was rooted in the blues. His 1956 version of "Blueberry Hill" used a 12/8 pattern of repeated triplet chords in the right hand and the slow blues left-hand pattern. Even though the song was not a 12-bar blues, it has entered the common blues repertoire. And blues musicians to this day call the pattern of repeated triplet chords in the right hand with the slow-blues left hand the "Blueberry Hill" style. Example 1 has tremolos in the right hand instead of repeated chords.

EXAMPLE 1

TRACK 22
0:00
CD 2

Domino used the triplet rhythm in his right hand often. Example 2 *begins* with the "Blues Ending" and then goes into the repeated triplets in the right hand.

EXAMPLE 2

TRACK 22
0:19
CD 2

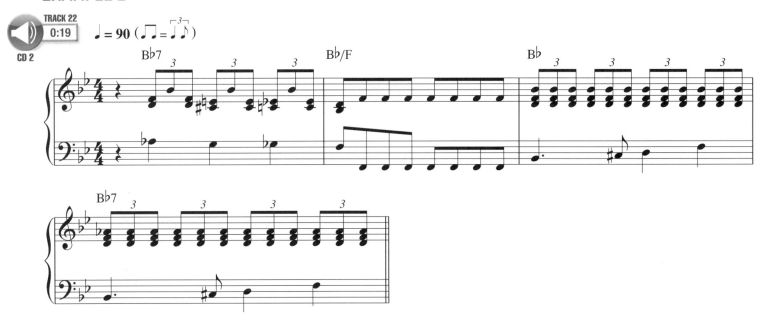

Domino often used a fast two-handed shuffle pattern.

EXAMPLE 3

TRACK 22 0:34 CD 2

He also used a medium shuffle rhythm with a walking bass line, similar to a standard jump blues pattern, although not quite as fast.

EXAMPLE 4

TRACK 22 0:42 CD 2

At times, Domino used the barrelhouse left-hand pattern played in eighth notes. Example 5 also has tremolos in the right hand.

EXAMPLE 5

TRACK 22 0:50 CD 2

Nearly all of Domino's music was blues-based.

LESSON #73: THE B3 BLUES

A book of lessons on blues keyboard focuses mainly on the piano. But blues pianists can learn a lot from our brothers and sisters who play the **Hammond B3 organ**.

The Hammond organ was first manufactured in the 1930s and the B3 model was introduced in 1954. It became enormously popular with jazz musicians such as Jimmy Smith, Jack McDuff, and Booker T. Jones. Nearly all the players known for their B3 skills are adept at blues.

The sound of a Hammond organ is varied through the manipulation of drawbars. It also has characteristic Chorus and Leslie effects. The B3 sound can more or less be duplicated by today's digital keyboards, but organists like the vintage equipment for its authentic timbre and seek out old equipment to refurbish.

Jimmy Smith (1925–2005) was a jazz organist who recorded dozens of albums between 1956 and 2001. Much of his music was based on the 12-bar blues. His best known song is "Back at the Chicken Shack," a 12-bar blues in F that features 3rds in the right hand and a tremolo over a walking bass line. Example 1 is in the style of that tune.

EXAMPLE 1

Play any of the many turnarounds on that tune and it will be a lesson in effective chord voicing. Here's one.

EXAMPLE 2

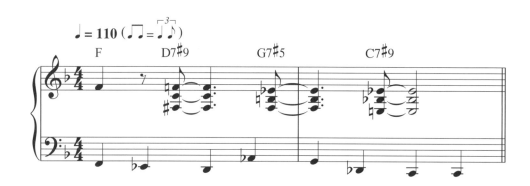

Smith played a solo chorus in "Chicken Shack" in which he played a series of 3rds in a triplet rhythm in his right hand. The rhythm becomes displaced in a very funky and effective manner.

EXAMPLE 3

Booker T. Jones (born in Memphis in 1944) is known for being the leader of Booker T. and the M.G.s. His most famous recording is the minor blues "Green Onions." The song is a 12-bar blues in F minor. The main chords are Fm, B♭, and C. However, there is a riff on each bar that makes each chord into three chords. The Fm chord becomes Fm, A♭, and B♭ chords. The B♭ chord becomes B♭, D♭, and E♭ chords. The C major chord turns into C, E♭, and F chords. Example 4 is the first four bars, which would normally just be on an F minor chord, but the riff is Fm, A♭, and B♭.

EXAMPLE 4

When the melody of the tune actually begins, the bass walks the chord pattern.

EXAMPLE 5

Check out B3 players. Other players worth looking into include "Brother" Jack McDuff, Jimmy McGriff, and Joey DeFrancesco.

LESSON #74: RIFF BLUES

A particular category of blues melodic form is the **riff blues**, in which the same melodic riff appears throughout the 12-bar blues form, with no variations.

The most famous example of this is Duke Ellington's "C Jam Blues," one of the simplest tunes ever written – it has two notes in the melody. However, only a genius like Ellington could take two notes and make them into a tune that swings and doesn't get boring. Not surprisingly, "C Jam Blues" is written in the key of C major. The two notes used in the melody are C (the tonic) and G (the dominant). A four-bar melodic phrase is played three times over the 12-bar chord sequence. Here are the first four bars:

EXAMPLE 1

Ellington's blues form in this song uses the I7 chord over bars 1–4, the iim7 in bar 9, and the V7 chord in bar 10. The tune is played in a very bright swing tempo and the bass almost always walks throughout. Example 2 has the piano playing the melody using four-note, two-handed, rootless chord voicings.

EXAMPLE 2

Another example of the riff blues is Sonny Rollins's tune "Sonnymoon for Two." It has a four-bar melody that is played three times verbatim in the 12-bar progression. Rollins's used the same chord progression that Ellington uses in "C Jam Blues." The example below is in the style of Rollins's tune. The melody is made up entirely of notes from the C minor blues scale. It is sometimes harmonized in the following manner, with every melodic note voiced as a 13th chord, with the 7th in the left hand.

EXAMPLE 3

Count Basie's "One O'Clock Jump" is a riff blues. It was the Count Basie Orchestra's theme song. The four-bar melodic pattern in Example 4 is in the style of Basie's tune. The pattern is played three times during the 12-bar progressions.

EXAMPLE 4

TRACK 24
0:28
CD 2

The song contains an additional one-bar riff that is played over the first 10 bars of the 12-bar sequence. Example 5 is in that style.

EXAMPLE 5

TRACK 24
0:36
CD 2

Familiarize yourself with these and other riff blues songs. If you make up your own blues melodies, remember that the riff blues is a simple, but effective, way to construct a blues tune.

LESSON #75: BEBOP BLUES

Thelonious Monk (1917–1982) was an American jazz pianist and composer who brought a highly original approach to jazz and blues. His piano style was full of dissonances, angular melodic twists, a very percussive attack, and abrupt silences. He wrote about 70 songs, many of which have become jazz standards. His two most famous tunes are both 12-bar blues: "Blue Monk" and "Straight No Chaser."

"Blue Monk" follows a standard 12-bar pattern using the V7 chord in both bars 9 and 10. Sometimes in **bebop blues** the IV7 chord in bar 5 is followed by the ♯ivdim7 chord in bar 6. The chord is created by replacing the root of IV7 with the blue note ♯4. Otherwise the chord notes are the same. This chord is optional in "Blue Monk," as some lead sheets of the song include it and some don't. Example 1 is in the style of "Blue Monk," beginning with a riff using parallel 3rds.

EXAMPLE 1

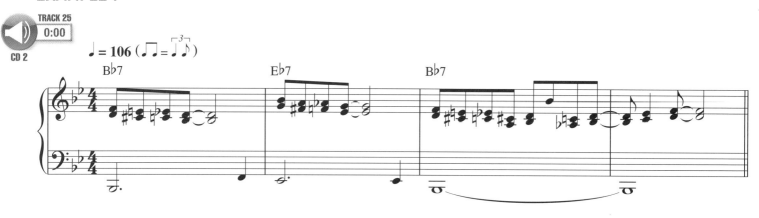

When performing the tune, Monk would often play the head by himself with very little left hand at all, except for a bass note punch here and there. Once the band kicked in on the second chorus, the bass would usually play walking patterns throughout.

"Straight No Chaser" featured the 12-bar progression, using the V7 chord in both bars 9 and 10, and a one-beat anticipation of the IV7 chord on the last beat of bar 4. Example 2 is in the style of that tune. It's based on a simple five-note riff. Note how the riff is rhythmically displaced throughout the first four bars. The tune is played here with tritone voicings in the left hand.

EXAMPLE 2

Monk was affiliated with Milt "Bags" Jackson (1923–1999), a great vibraphonist who was very fond of blues. The two performed Jackson's composition "Bag's Groove" while both were in Miles Davis's group. The tune is a **riff blues**, based on a four-bar riff that is played three times. The progression is fairly standard, although a VI7 chord is played in bar 8, the iim7 chord is played in bar 9, and the V7 chord is played in bar 10. Example 3 is in the style of Jackson's song. The melody is based on notes from the F minor blues scale and features a triplet turn in bars 1 and 2 that lies well for the fingers. The left hand in the example uses three-note rootless chord voicings.

EXAMPLE 3

The final example represents bars 5–8 in the "Blue Monk" style.

EXAMPLE 4

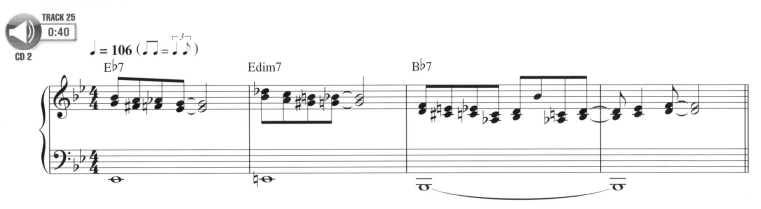

Listen to the way bebop players approach the blues.

LESSON #76: BLUES WALTZ

Blues isn't always in 4/4 time. We've seen that slow blues are often in 12/8 meter. However, medium-to-fast blues can also be played in 3/4 or 6/8 time. Example 1 shows the first eight bars of an original blues in 3/4 time. The left hand simply plays held chords voiced in an open position.

EXAMPLE 1

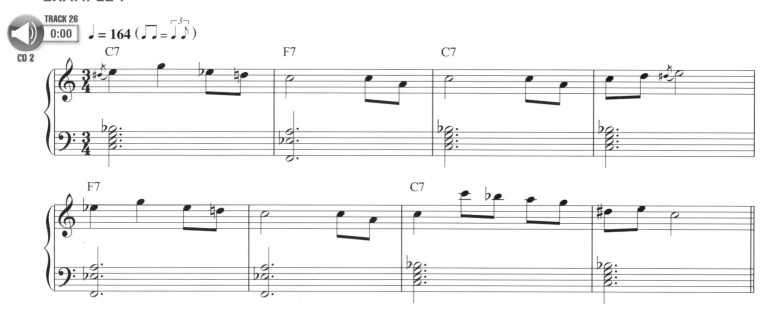

In a **blues waltz**, the number of bars is often doubled so that the piece becomes a 24-bar blues, instead of a 12-bar blues. A good example is the song "West Coast Blues" by guitarist Wes Montgomery. The next example presents the first four bars of a 24-bar blues waltz. These four bars would normally be just two bars. The example is based on a two-bar riff, which is then repeated in bars 3 and 4.

EXAMPLE 2

A well-known blues in 6/8 is "All Blues" by Miles Davis, which follows a 12-bar progression. The song is usually written in 6/8 with swung 16th notes. However, I prefer to think of "All Blues" in 3/4 time with double the number of measures, making it a 24-bar blues. The song has a familiar bass line and right-hand piano chords that continue throughout the song.

EXAMPLE 3

Blues in 3/4 time can be played with the **jazz waltz** left-hand pattern shown below. Of course, you can also incorporate any of the other techniques discussed herein into a blues waltz

EXAMPLE 4

Learn some blues in 3/4 time. Add some variety to your blues tunes.

LESSON #77: THE GOSPEL/BLUES LINK

The musical genres of gospel, jazz, blues, and boogie-woogie all arose at about the same time and from the same influences. The time period was approximately the 1880s through the 1920s. The styles were the result of interaction between blacks of African descent, with their African music influences, and white Americans with their primarily European musical influences.

In southern ports like New Orleans, considered to be the birthplace of jazz, there were also Caribbean musical influences. Jelly Roll Morton referred to these influences as The Spanish Tinge.

Black gospel music grew out of the negro spirituals created by African slaves, who fused African music and religion with the traditional Christianity and hymns of the slave owners. Spirituals are ubiquitous in our society. Nearly everyone is familiar with songs like "He's Got the Whole World in His Hands," "Kum Ba Yah," and "When the Saints Go Marching In."

Because of their similar roots, there's a lot of crossover in the genres of **gospel** and **blues**. Some even claim that you can take any blues tune and make it into a gospel tune by substituting the word "God" for the word "baby" and vice versa. When you examine the titles of spirituals, it becomes clear that many of them are blues: "Sometimes I Feel Like a Motherless Child," "Nobody Knows the Trouble I've Seen," or "Deep River."

"When the Saints Go Marching In" is a spiritual that's also become a jazz standard. When played by a Dixieland jazz band, it's usually played as a bright swing tune with a walking bass.

EXAMPLE 1

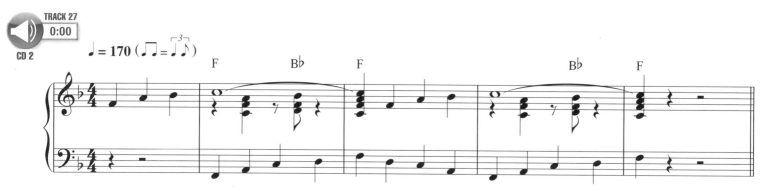

It's also commonly played in a bluesier stride style.

EXAMPLE 2

Dr. John plays the tune in a New Orleans **funeral romp style**, with straight eighths. It's close to a boogie-woogie.

EXAMPLE 3

"Amazing Grace" is a traditional hymn that lends itself well to a gospel/blues treatment. Example 4 presents the first few bars of "Amazing Grace." It uses some blue notes and embellishing chords. The first chord temporarily moves to the chord with a root an interval of a 4th higher and then returns to the first chord. This I-IV technique is very common in gospel piano styles and in blues.

EXAMPLE 4

Example 5 shows a two-bar into and two bars of "This Little Light of Mine" in a bluesy stride style.

EXAMPLE 5

LESSON #78: THE GOSPEL/BLUES LINK II

This lesson continues the connection between **gospel** and **blues** music. While most spirituals or gospel songs are not 12-bar blues, such songs are generally played with a blues feeling and often incorporate standard blues keyboard techniques.

"Down by the Riverside" is a spiritual that can be played in a swing fashion. However, the version in Example 1 uses straight eighths with a sort of boogie-woogie left hand.

EXAMPLE 1

"What a Friend We Have in Jesus" can be played with a stride left hand with moving chords in the right hand and succinct right hand fills, such as in bar 4.

EXAMPLE 2

Jazz pianist Ramsey Lewis often played in a neo-gospel style. His version of the spiritual "Wade in the Water" featured a straight-eighths groove in the key of D minor.

EXAMPLE 3

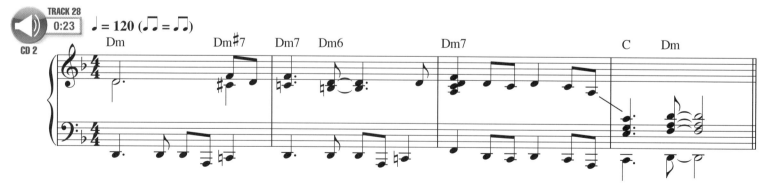

Example 4 is another Ramsey Lewis gospel groove in straight eighths. Like a standard blues, it uses all dominant 7th chords, including one on the ♭VII (E♭9) degree of the key of F.

EXAMPLE 4

Finally, here's a little bit of the spiritual "Sometimes I Feel Like a Motherless Child." It's done in 3/4 time in the key of D minor, with lots of grace notes sliding into the melody notes.

EXAMPLE 5

Other gospel/blues pianists to check out include Ray Charles and Aretha Franklin. On her early recordings, Ms. Franklin dynamically accompanied herself on piano.

LESSON #79: IDEAS FOR IMPROVISATION

This lesson focuses on some general ideas for sparking your blues improvisations.

First, leave **space** (rests) in your music. You don't have to fill up each space with notes. It's better to have too little happening than too much. In Example 1, there is lots of space between the musical ideas. The example also illustrates the idea of using both **steps** and **leaps**. The descending octave leaps are very effective.

EXAMPLE 1

Use **repeated notes**. You don't have to follow a note with a different note. Sometimes the same note will do. Repetition is one of the most fundamental characteristics of the blues. Try using **just a few notes** and do a lot with them, instead of doing little with a lot of notes. A good player can make an entire solo out of a few notes. Example 2 uses just two melodic notes, G and F♯.

EXAMPLE 2

Play in **different registers** of the piano. This is an effective way to change the tone color and the texture. Example 3 begins with the right hand playing in the upper register of the piano, but in bars 2 and 3 the right hand quickly descends into the bass clef and the left hand takes over and goes even lower.

EXAMPLE 3

TRACK 29
0:23
CD 2

Make mistakes. Don't be afraid to take risks. In a sense, there are no wrong notes. When you hit a note that seems out of place or clashes with the chord, you can always correct the note and it will sound like it was planned that way. Furthermore, you could even repeat the mistake and then correct it. For instance, in the next example the E♮ in bar 2 over the F7 chord seems wrong, but it is quickly corrected in the same bar. Then, the wrong note is basically repeated over the C7 chord in bar 3.

EXAMPLE 4

TRACK 29
0:34
CD 2

Finally, **learn from the masters.** It is wrong to think that you must reinvent the wheel. In music, we build on the work of those who have gone before us. All original composers and performers began with imitation. Imitation is one of the best ways to learn.

Go hear **live performances.** Listen to **recorded music** you enjoy and try to reproduce it on the keyboard. Also, **record yourself** and determine what areas of your playing need to be improved.

LESSON #80: 16-BAR BLUES

The blues doesn't always have to be 12-bars. The **16-bar blues**, an adaptation from the 12-bar form, is also popular. A good example is Herbie Hancock's tune "Watermelon Man," a funky, straight-eighths blues first recorded in 1962. The song follows a standard blues progression, except that bars 9 and 10 of the 12-bar form are played three times, making it 16 bars in all. The progression is given below.

EXAMPLE 1

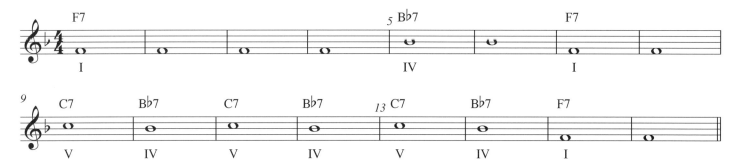

The song has a one-bar introduction riff that is generally played four to eight times as the intro.

EXAMPLE 2

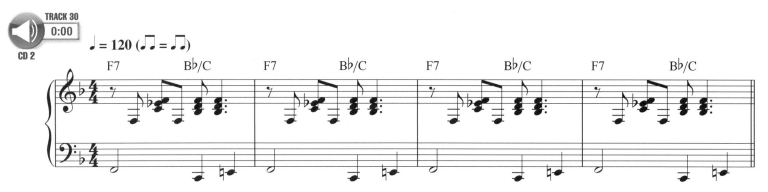

Another kind of 16-bar blues is typified by Willie Dixon's "I'm Your Hoochie Coochie Man." The first four bars of the tonic chord are extended to eight bars. The rest of the 12-bar progression remains the same. The first eight bars use a standard blues lead-in riff that leads to the downbeat of each bar. Other than the downbeat, the remainder of each bar is filled by the vocal, with no instrumental other than drums. Example 3 features three different variations of the lead-in riff.

EXAMPLE 3

Typically, in bar 8 the entire band comes in for the rest of the form. Example 4 begins with the lead-in to bar 8. In this style of blues, the piano generally plays repeated chords in a triplet rhythm in the right hand, while the left hand uses a walking bass:

EXAMPLE 4

TRACK 30
0:38
CD 2

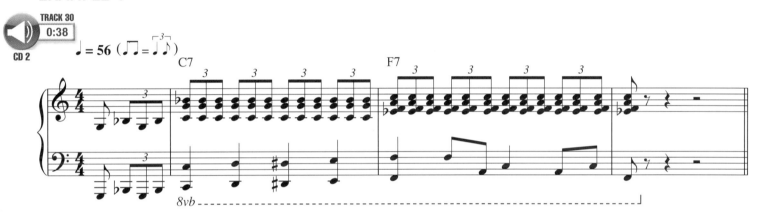

There are other kinds of 16-bar blues, but the two versions above are the most common. One features an extension of bars 9 and 10 of the 12-bar blues. The other utilizes an extension of the first bars of the 12-bar blues.

LESSON #81: DEVELOPING A MELODIC RIFF

This lesson looks at how a simple blues riff can be developed in various ways to make it into a complete 12-bar melody.

First, a riff can be **repeated verbatim** or with slight changes. Example 1 takes a riff similar to one found in "Pinetop's Boogie-Woogie." The riff is repeated verbatim in each of the first four bars, except that the notes are slightly altered to fit the F7 chord in bar 2.

EXAMPLE 1

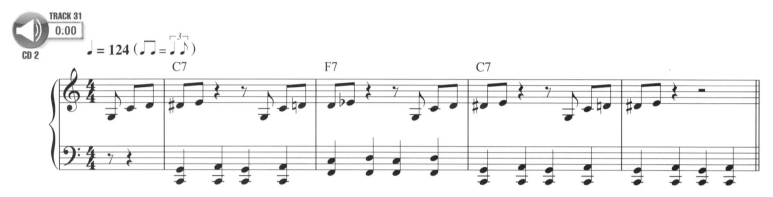

One could also **play the riff in sequence**, i.e., repeat the riff at a higher or lower pitch level. Example 2 uses the same melodic riff, which is played a 4th higher over the F7 chord in bar 2.

EXAMPLE 2

Rhythmically, one could also lengthen the note values of the riff (**augmentation**) or shorten the rhythmic values (**diminution**).

A further rhythmic technique is called **rhythmic displacement**. This is a technique where the notes of the riff are the same, but the riff begins at a different place in the bar. The next example has rhythmic displacement in bars 3 and 4.

EXAMPLE 3

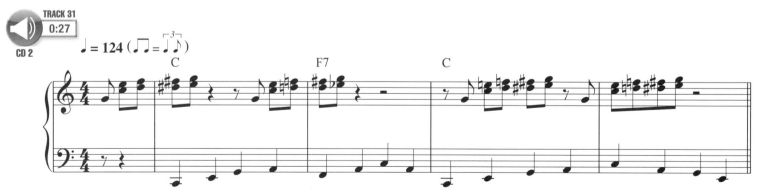

One could take the riff and break it into fragments, or omit notes or add notes. Other possibilities include changing the intervals, turning the riff upside down (**inversion**) or playing it backward (**retrograde**).

The final example in this lesson illustrates the use of a two-beat descending riff that is played and then notes are added.

EXAMPLE 4

JOHNNIE JOHNSON STYLE

Johnnie Johnson (1924–2005) played piano for Chuck Berry from 1955 to 1973. He was inducted into the Rock and Roll Hall of Fame in 2001.

In 1952, Johnson lived in St. Louis and fronted a blues band. When he needed a last-minute replacement, he hired the very young guitarist Chuck Berry. Berry ended up playing with the band for several years. At some point, Berry submitted one of the band's tunes to Chess Records. When Chess signed Berry to a solo recording contract, the tables turned and Johnson became a member of Berry's band.

Johnson played with Berry on most of Berry's classic early rock recordings. Later, Johnson recorded albums under his own name, including 1991's "Johnnie B. Bad," on which both Eric Clapton and Keith Richards played.

Johns was fond of the key of G and liked the barrelhouse left-hand played in eighth notes.

EXAMPLE 1

Occasionally, he'd use a left-hand bass in walking octaves.

EXAMPLE 2

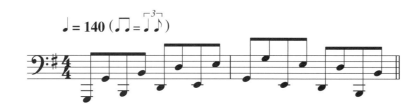

Johnson's most famous solo recording is the medium-tempo shuffle "Tanqueray," on which he displayed his bag of tricks.

EXAMPLE 3

Johnson liked a particular lick over the V7 chord in bar 9 and the IV7 in chord in bar 10:

EXAMPLE 4

He also liked to use a particular lick over the IV7 chord in bars 5 and 6:

EXAMPLE 5

Of course, Johnson was best known for his work with Chuck Berry. Example 6 is a straight-eighths rock riff similar to Berry's "Johnny B. Goode," which was named in honor of Johnnie Johnson, even though the name is spelled differently.

EXAMPLE 6

Marcia Ball (b. 1949) is a blues singer/pianist who grew up in Louisiana, but who's lived most of her life in Austin, Texas. Her blues style is generally a mixture of New Orleans influences and Texas blues. She's talked about being influenced by Professor Longhair, so it's not surprising that one of her most popular songs is her rendition of Professor Longhair's "Red Beans."

"Red Beans" is a fast, straight-eighths blues with a boogie-like left hand. Example 1 is in the style of Ball's version.

EXAMPLE 1

The solo licks Ball uses on "Red Beans" are largely pentatonic, with grace notes slides into the 3rd of the G chord.

EXAMPLE 2

Ball also performs a straight-eighths boogie rendition of "Route 66." The basic riff she uses is shown in the next example. Note that the major 3rd and the minor 3rd are alternated in the riff in the right hand.

EXAMPLE 3

Ball's version of "Let Me Play with Your Poodle" is taken at a breakneck speed. (It's demonstrated at a fairly moderate 150 beats per minute on Track 33.) The eighth notes are swung, so it seems – it's hard to even tell at Ball's tempo. The song begins with an octave unison lick using the notes of the C minor blues scale. When the IV chord is played at bar 3, the left hand kicks in with a barrelhouse pattern. Meanwhile, a horn riff is doubled by the right hand of the piano.

EXAMPLE 4

Marcia Ball has been tearing it up on the piano for years. She's a great singer, too.

LESSON #84: JIMMY YANCEY STYLE

Jimmy Yancey (1898–1951) was a Chicago blues pianist who was a pioneer of the boogie-woogie style. Yancey had a job outside music: For 25 years he was a groundskeeper for the Chicago White Sox baseball team at their home stadium in Chicago's Comiskey Park. Yancey's house was a gathering place for Chicago blues and boogie-woogie pianists, including Meade Lux Lewis, Albert Ammons, and Clarence "Pinetop" Smith.

Yancey's "State Street Special" used a somewhat unusual left-hand pattern. The turnaround figure in bars 11 and 12 is still played by pianists today.

EXAMPLE 1

The song also has a great ending, using the E♭ minor blues scale.

EXAMPLE 2

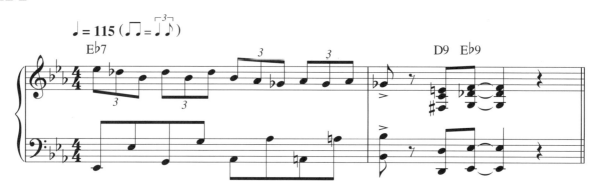

Yancey popularized a left-hand figure that became known as the **Yancey bass.** It was a three-note syncopated rhythm – the first note and the last note fall on the beat, but the middle note is offbeat. This bass was later used by New Orleans pianist Professor Longhair who based his "Rumba Boogie" beat on it. Professor Longhair complicated the figure a bit by adding a few notes and including a grace note on the syncopated note. You should play the grace note – and the syncopated note that it slides into – with the middle finger of the left hand.

EXAMPLE 3

Yancey was also known for employing parallel 3rds and parallel 6ths in the right hand.

EXAMPLE 4

TRACK 34
0:30
CD 2

Yancey was instrumental in the development of boogie-woogie in the late 1920s. He influenced Pinetop Smith and Meade Lux Lewis, but he himself didn't record until the 1930s.

LESSON #85: MEMPHIS SLIM STYLE

Memphis Slim (1915–1988) was born John Chatman in Memphis, Tennessee. He was self-taught and became a wandering musician for many years, before settling down in Chicago in 1939. His 1947 song "Every Day I Have the Blues" is an important blues standard. He published songs under the *nom de plume* Peter Chatman, his father's name. In 1961 he moved to Paris, where he lived until his death. In France, he was treated as a blues demigod, being chauffeured around in a Rolls Royce.

Memphis Slim used standard patterns in his left hand, such as the barrelhouse pattern (a), the eighth-note barrelhouse pattern (b), and various boogie-woogie patterns (c).

EXAMPLE 1

In his right hand, Memphis Slim was fond of fast single-note runs based primarily on the minor blues scale. He often used tremolos in the right hand.

EXAMPLE 2

He also liked using parallel 3rds and 6ths in his right hand. Note the parallel 3rds played as tremolos in Example 3.

EXAMPLE 3

TRACK 35
0:32
CD 2

Observe that in the example above, Memphis Slim simplified the left hand a bit.

LESSON #86: CHARLES "COW COW" DAVENPORT STYLE

Charles "Cow Cow" Davenport (1894–1955) was born in Anniston, Alabama. He learned to play piano at his father's church. It looked like he was following his father into the ministry until he was expelled from the Alabama Theological Seminary in 1911 for playing ragtime on the seminary's piano. He then took up the life of a traveling medicine show musician, performing throughout the South with his wife, who was a snake charmer.

Davenport moved to Chicago in the 1920s and got his nickname from his song "Cow Cow Blues," which he recorded in 1927. It's one of the earliest recorded examples of boogie-woogie piano. "Cow Cow Blues" is a standard of the blues piano repertoire and is the basis for Ray Charles's famous recording entitled "Mess Around."

"Cow Cow Blues" is played using straight eighths. It's a 12-bar blues, but the IV7 chord in bar 2 is skipped: I7 is played for the first four bars. Also, the IV7 chord in bar 10 is skipped: V7 is played in both bars 9 and 10. The bass walks in octaves.

EXAMPLE 1

Davenport uses a series of slides in the right hand that are intended to imitate a train whistle.

EXAMPLE 2

Davenport's signature is the phrase played in every chorus from bar 9 to bar 12. He played the same phrase in the song "Back in the Alley," which is very similar to "Cow Cow Blues."

EXAMPLE 3

Davenport also uses a syncopated passage in the right hand, using a series of three notes in a 16th-note rhythm.

EXAMPLE 4

LESSON #87: CLARENCE "PINETOP" SMITH STYLE

Clarence "Pinetop" Smith (1904–1929) was born and raised in Troy, Alabama. He got his nickname as a child for his penchant for climbing trees. He moved to Chicago in 1928 and exerted a huge influence on the boogie-woogie pianists Meade Lux Lewis and Albert Ammons. His "Pinetop's Boogie-Woogie" was recorded in 1928 and was the first recorded piece to use the term boogie-woogie in the title. Smith was accidently shot and killed during a fracas at a dancehall where he was performing in 1929. He was only 24 years old.

"Pinetop's Boogie-Woogie" established several basic conventions for piano boogie-woogies. After a tremolo introduction, the piece launches into its rollicking boogie-woogie feel in bar 7. The left hand boogie-woogie pattern remains the same for the entire piece.

EXAMPLE 1

The right hand begins with a riff, repeated verbatim seven times. The riff used grace notes and emphasized the minor 3rd of the tonic chord sliding into the major 3rd.

EXAMPLE 2

The pattern in the right hand based on 3rds has become a standard blues/boogie riff.

EXAMPLE 3

TRACK 37
0:19
CD 2

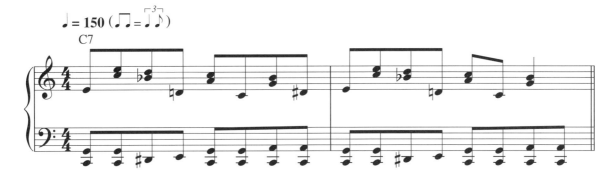

At bar 37, there's a right-hand rhythmic chordal section where the right hand simply plays two block chords every bar in a syncopated, punchy rhythm. Such rhythmic chordal sections became common in boogie-woogies. In the 1928 recording, Pinetop speaks lyrics describing the dance moves. The words sound quite contemporary: "Hey, little girl with the red dress on. I want you to shake that thing." The spoken-word convention is popular in hip-hop and rap to this day.

EXAMPLE 4

TRACK 37
0:27
CD 2

Finally, there's a break at bar 49 for the first four bars of the 12-bar chorus. The bass line stops and the two hands play a two-handed tremolo, and then a melody in two-handed octaves, which eventually goes back into the boogie-woogie feel in bar 5 of the chorus. Such breaks have become commonplace.

EXAMPLE 5

TRACK 37
0:37
CD 2

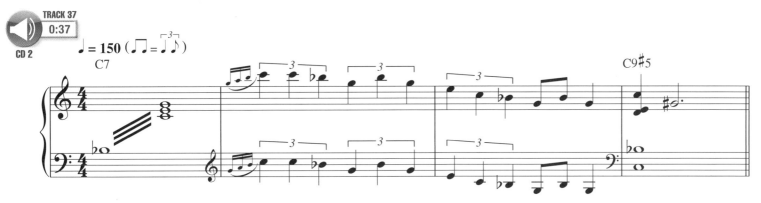

Even though Pinetop Smith only lived to be 24, he established the conventions for the boogie-woogies that were recorded after him.

Charles Brown (1922–1999) was born in Galveston, Texas. He studied classical piano, had a college degree in chemistry, and taught school for a short time. In the mid-1940s he moved to Los Angeles, where he freelanced as a pianist. Brown was influenced by the piano style and gentle vocal style of Nat "King" Cole. His biggest hit was called "Driftin' Blues" (1945). Brown had retired by the 1980s, but Bonnie Raitt included him as the opening act on her 1990 tour, reviving his career.

Brown played in a laid-back and relaxed manner, known as the West Coast Style. In Example 1, note the left-hand voicings that Brown used, which are characteristic of the rootless chord voicings found in modern jazz piano. The I chord, which would normally be played as a 7th chord, is voiced as a 13th chord and the IV chord is played as a 9th. The chords are articulated in a punchy, syncopated rhythm.

EXAMPLE 1

In his right hand, Brown used licks based on 3rds. He also played sparser chord voicings in the left hand, just two-note voicings.

EXAMPLE 2

Brown ends this particular performance with his own variation of the "Ellington ending."

EXAMPLE 3

Brown had several hit songs that were in a slow 12/8 meter, including "Driftin' Blues," "Merry Christmas, Baby," and "Please Come Home for Christmas." His characteristic licks in "Driftin' Blues" are shown here:

EXAMPLE 4

LESSON #89: JAMES BOOKER STYLE

James Booker (1939–1983) was a New Orleans pianist who combined blues, stride, jazz, gospel, and classical training into his style. Dr. John described Booker as "the best black, gay, one-eyed junkie piano genius New Orleans has ever produced."

Booker's peers called him "The Piano Prince of New Orleans," but his life was a study in struggle. At one point, he lost his left eye. (There are various stories about how this happened.) He had serious problems with heroin and cocaine, was mentally ill, and spent time in prison. He died at the age of 43 in the emergency ward of Charity Hospital.

Booker didn't play 12-bar blues often, but all his playing was infused with blues. He played stride with a unique left hand. He put extra, bluesy figures that alternated the major and minor 3rds on the "ands" of beats 2 and 4, instead of just playing chords on each beat.

EXAMPLE 1

In his right hand, Booker often played full four-note block chords when playing stride.

EXAMPLE 2

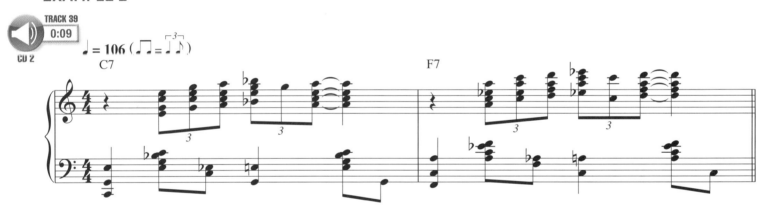

Booker showed a bluesy, funky straight-eighths style on "Junko Partner," in which he emphasized both the minor and major 3rds of the chord.

EXAMPLE 3

In the boogie-woogie shuffle "Tell Me How Do You Feel," instead of just playing a typical boogie-woogie figure in the left hand, Booker added notes to the figure to create a fuller sound. When played with two hands, the basic boogie-woogie figure is fairly difficult to play.

EXAMPLE 4

TRACK 39
0:26
CD 2

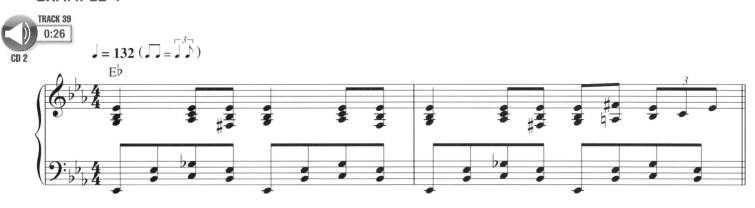

Example 5 is the full Booker groove on "Tell Me How Do You Feel."

EXAMPLE 5

TRACK 39
0:33
CD 2

LESSON #90: GENE HARRIS STYLE

Gene Harris (1933–2000) was a jazz pianist who blended blues, gospel, and jazz into a style sometimes called **soul jazz**.

Harris's version of the spiritual "This Little Light of Mine" was a straight-eighths boogie-woogie in the key of F. It's not a 12-bar blues, but a 16-bar piece. Following a short, free-form intro, Harris established the left-hand boogie-woogie pattern, a sort of upside-down version of the eighth-note barrelhouse pattern. It's played at about 140 bpm. Harris used a lot of parallel 6ths in the right-hand melody.

EXAMPLE 1

A turnaround is used throughout the piece.

EXAMPLE 2

Near the end, there's a free-form piano break, then a four-bar ending in a slower tempo, about 80 bpm. The left-hand part for the ending is a fairly standard ascending bass line. The piece ends with a C7#9 chord, a nice voicing of an F13 chord, and some quick glissandos – going up, then back down, then up again.

EXAMPLE 3

Example 4 is Harris's piano groove on his "Down Home Blues." It's taken at a fairly slow 72 bpm.

EXAMPLE 4

TRACK 40
0:34
CD 2

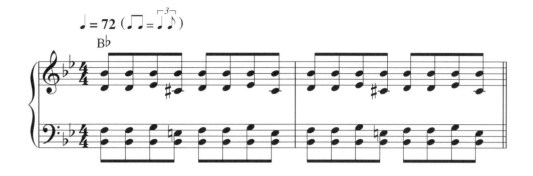

Check out recordings by Gene Harris. His blues-oriented jazz style was very appealing.

LESSON #91: STRIDE-STYLE BLUES

Blues has often been played in **stride style**. In fact, almost all early blues were played that way. Many players throughout the years have played stride-style blues, including Count Basie. Stride-style piano generally is characterized by an "oom-pah" or "boom-chuck" left hand. There is usually a bass note on beat 1, followed by a chord in close position on beat 2, followed by another bass note on beat 3, followed by a chord on beat 4.

James P. Johnson (in the 1920s), Fats Waller (in the 1930s), and Art Tatum (in the 1940s) were all masters of stride. Stride can be virtuosic and very entertaining. It's quite a challenge for the left hand.

Stride has its roots in ragtime. Ragtime took its "oom-pah" left hand from marches by John Philip Sousa (1854–1932) and others. Example 1 is in the style of Scott Joplin's "Paragon Rag" (1909). Ragtime was generally written in 2/4 rather than 4/4. Just think of each eighth note in 2/4 as being one beat, like a quarter note in 4/4. By the way, ragtime is never supposed to be played fast. Joplin wrote that instruction on nearly every rag he published. Ragtime should be played at a leisurely walking/marching pace.

EXAMPLE 1

TRACK 41
0:00
CD 2

Examples 2–6 all use the classic blues melody "St. Louis Blues" in the key of G. "St Louis Blues" was written by W.C. Handy and is now in the public domain. Example 2 has the basic melody played by the right hand and a typical stride pattern in the left.

EXAMPLE 2

TRACK 41
0:11
CD 2

Another left-hand technique common in stride-style piano is walking triads, as shown in Example 3. Notice how the triads start on a G chord, walk up to a C chord, then walk back down to the G chord. Meanwhile, the right hand plays the melody and fills in with blues licks in bars 3 and 4.

EXAMPLE 3

Example 4 mixes the left-hand techniques. There are walking triads in bar 1, triads followed by a higher chord in bar 2, walking triads in bar 3, and a traditional stride pattern in bar 4. The right hand gets much bluesier, with a repeated lick in bar 1 and blues fills in bars 3 and 4.

EXAMPLE 4

Here we have a stride pattern in bar 1 and an ending bit in bars 3 and 4:

EXAMPLE 5

LESSON #92: BLUES BALLAD

A **blues ballad** is a song in a slow tempo that doesn't necessarily follow a 12-bar blues form. It is performed in a bluesy manner and often has entered the standard blues repertoire. Most often, a blues ballad is a jazz standard in a 32-bar format. An example is "Georgia on My Mind," a standard written by Hoagy Carmichael that has become a staple in the blues repertoire. Other examples are "Since I Fell For You," "Cry Me a River," "Blueberry Hill," "God Bless' the Child," "At Last," "Stormy Weather," and even George Gershwin's "Summertime."

These songs are generally sung, but instrumental versions are also popular. Blues ballads are almost always played with swing-eighth notes, which gives the songs a slow 12/8 feel. "Georgia on My Mind" is customarily played with the standard slow blues left-hand pattern, as shown in Example 1.

EXAMPLE 1

"At Last," "Stormy Weather," and "Since I Fell for You" are all based on the I-vi-ii-V "Blue Moon" progression. The songs are usually played with a constant pattern of triplets in the right hand. The "Blue Moon" progression looks like this:

EXAMPLE 2

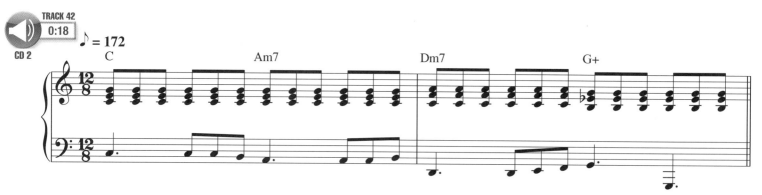

Here's another way to play the "Blue Moon" progression:

EXAMPLE 3

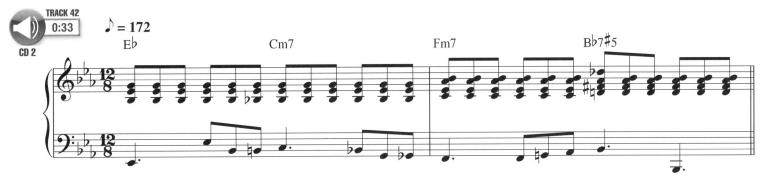

Both "Cry Me a River" and "Good Morning Heartache" are in a minor key with a progression in the first two bars that features a chromatically ascending inner line – the 5th of the chord rises chromatically. The progression lends itself well to piano.

EXAMPLE 4

The song "Black Coffee" may be the bluesiest of the blues ballads. It features the alternation of the I7#9 chord with the same chord a half step higher.

EXAMPLE 5

Blues ballads are not in a 12-bar blues format, but are a staple part of the standard blues repertoire. Familiarize yourself with them.

LESSON #93: PLAYING IN A BLUES BAND

Backing up a singer or soloist in a combo is known as **comping**, which is short for accompanying. Comping involves chordal playing and occasionally adding fills between vocal or melodic phrases. Rather than solo improvisation, what's important in comping is to keep the rhythm and harmony going and to complement the soloist, not compete with them.

Often in a combo situation, keyboard comping chords are played with both hands together in rhythmic patterns that are punchy and syncopated. The bass player in the combo will handle all the bass lines, so the comping chords are generally rootless chord voicings.

For instance, here's a comping pattern known as the **Charleston rhythm** for the first four bars of a blues in C. The chords are five-note rootless chord voicings, spread between the two hands. The voicings sound quite full.

EXAMPLE 1

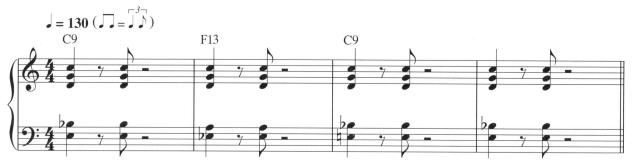

Example 2 shows comping rhythm for the last four bars of a 12-bar progression. Bars 2 and 4 use the same rhythm, but the other bars have different rhythms.

EXAMPLE 2

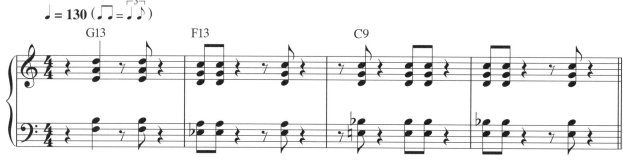

Example 3 uses the Charleston rhythm in bars 1 and 2, but employs a different rhythm in bars 3 and 4.

EXAMPLE 3

Here's a comping rhythm for two bars that uses a boogie-woogie pattern in the left hand:

EXAMPLE 4

TRACK 43
0:33
CD 2

You should also know the typical comping rhythm for a slow blues in 12/8:

EXAMPLE 5

TRACK 43
0:41
CD 2

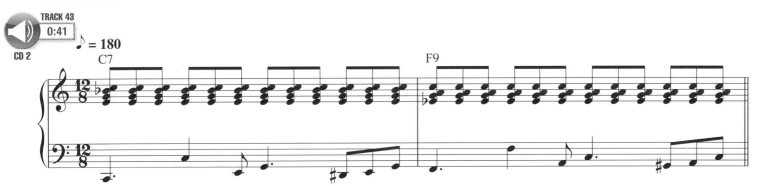

LESSON #94: NEW ORLEANS & THE RUMBA BOOGIE

Blues pianist and singer **Professor Longhair** (Henry Roeland Byrd, 1918–1980) was known as The Godfather of New Orleans Piano. Affectionately called "Fess," every New Orleans pianist after him has acknowledged his influence, especially Dr. John and Allen Toussaint.

One of the most significant things Fess did was to take a syncopated bass line, similar to Jimmy Yancey's bass line, and to turn it into a beat commonly known as the **rumba boogie**. This beat blended Afro-Cuban and Caribbean influences with the blues. The beat is typified below, played in straight eighths in a moderately slow tempo.

EXAMPLE 1

Example 2 lays out a few right hand licks that Professor Longhair would play over the rumba boogie beat.

EXAMPLE 2

Example 3 is a slight variation of the beat, with no syncopated notes in the left hand. Bar 4 is considered a standard New Orleans walk-up from the I chord to the IV chord. The right hand plays a pattern of octaves in 16th notes outlining a C major chord. The 16th notes are played in groups of three, and the left hand follows this syncopated rhythm with rhythmic punches. Dr. John and others still play this walk-up.

EXAMPLE 3

The rumba boogie can also be played with swing eighths. In Example 4, Professor Longhair begins with a rumba boogie bass line and then suddenly launches into a barrelhouse left-hand pattern.

EXAMPLE 4

Finally, the bass line can be spiced up with a sliding grace note or two. Example 5, a rumba boogie shuffle in a bright rhythm, uses grace notes to slide into the second bass note in each bar. The octaves are played with fingers 1 and 5, and the grace notes can also use fingers 1 and 5 to slide into the notes.

EXAMPLE 5

Professor Longhair's importance in blues seems to grow with time. Listen to his recordings.

OSCAR PETERSON – JAZZY BLUES, BLUESY JAZZ

Oscar Peterson (1925–2007) was one of the greatest jazz pianists ever. His career lasted 60 years. His greatest recordings were with his trio, either piano/bass/drums or piano/guitar/bass. However, Peterson was also an outstanding soloist. He had prodigious technique, but he also played with a great swing feeling and always infused his music with blues.

He often incorporated boogie-woogie into his playing. On "Oscar's Boogie," he plays at the ridiculously fast speed of 250 bpm. We've slowed it down to about 200 bpm. His left hand combined boogie-woogie figures, a standard boogie-woogie pattern, and walking octaves.

EXAMPLE 1

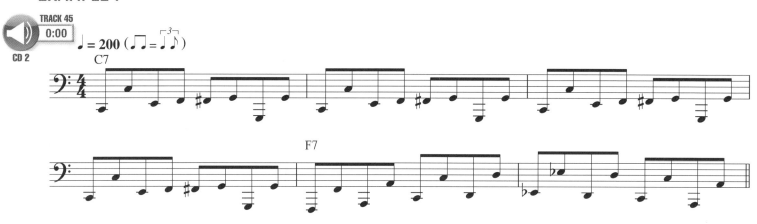

His melody was in typical boogie-woogie fashion, featuring parallel 3rds.

EXAMPLE 2

When it came time for a bass solo in the song, Peterson comped using two-handed chord voicings consisting of five or six notes, played in a syncopated, punchy rhythm.

EXAMPLE 3

Example 4 illustrates another Peterson technique: a repeated one-bar lick in the right hand, with walking octaves in the left.

EXAMPLE 4

Peterson devised a clever ending for this piece, using the ♭II6/9 chord resolving into the I 6/9 chord.

EXAMPLE 5

Any blues pianist can learn a thing or two from Oscar Peterson.

LESSON #96: POPULAR MELODIES IN A BOOGIE STYLE

It's fun to make up your own boogie-woogies. Also, most popular tunes can be adapted and played in a boogie-woogie style. You play the melody with the right hand, either in single notes or chords, while the left hand plays a boogie-woogie pattern that can be chosen from the dozens of standard figures.

The chords for a boogie-woogie typically follow the 12-bars blues. But when playing a popular tune in a boogie style, just take the chords from the lead sheet or sheet music of the song. The left-hand boogie-woogie figure follows the chords of the song. Songs with fewer chord changes work better than songs with lots of chord changes. Also, you must decide whether you want to play the song with swing-eighth notes or with straight-eighth notes.

Perhaps the most famous boogie-woogie that's based on a popular song is "Swanee River Boogie," based on Stephen Foster's "Old Folks at Home." "Swanee River Boogie" has been a featured song in the repertoire of Dr. John, Albert Ammons, and Fats Domino, among others.

The chords for "Swanee River Boogie" do not follow a 12-bar blues pattern, but the chords are all I, IV, and V. The bass line is a standard boogie-woogie figure. It just starts playing and the melody comes in whenever ready. The melody in bars 2–5 below covers the part of the tune with the words "Way down upon the Swanee River." Note that the melody is not played rhythmically straight, but instead is embellished with syncopation and extra notes. The way you play the melody is a matter of personal taste and feel.

EXAMPLE 1

TRACK 46
0:00
CD 2

Be selective when choosing the song you make into a boogie-woogie. Some of the tunes that have worked for me are ""This Little Light of Mine," "When the Saints Go Marching In," and "Down By the Riverside."

The well-known "Ode to Joy" from Beethoven's Symphony No. 9 works as a boogie-woogie theme. This, of course, was sung as "Joyful, Joyful, We Adore Thee" in the movie *Sister Act*. The song has a few more chord changes than are ideal, but it works pretty well as a straight-eighths boogie-woogie.

EXAMPLE 2

LESSON #97: BIRD BLUES

In the mid 1940s jazz musicians developed a new style called **bebop**. Virtuoso players such as alto saxophonist **Charlie Parker** and trumpeter **Dizzy Gillespie** played increasingly complicated chord progressions and tunes. Parker loved to play blues, but he introduced a chord sequence, using tritone substitution and chromatic chord changes, that was barely recognizable as blues. His blues chord progression has come to be known as "Bird Blues," after his nickname "Bird." It's also sometimes called "New York Changes."

Here is Parker's progression, given in Roman numerals:
Imaj7/viim7♭5-III7/vi7-V7/vm7-I7/IV7/ivm7-♭VII7/iiim7-VI7/♭iii-♭VI7/iim7-V7/iiim7-vim7/ii-V7

In the key of F, this translates into the following chords:
Fmaj7/Em7♭5-A7/Dm7-G7/Cm7-F7/B♭7/B♭m7-E♭7/Am7-D7/A♭m7-D♭7/Gm7-C7/Am7-Dm7/Gm7-C7

The chords basically use a cycle of descending ii-V progressions. Parker used these changes in his song "Blues for Alice." (The progression is also the basis for Toots Thieleman's "Bluesette.") Example 1 is in the style of the first five bars of "Blues for Alice."

EXAMPLE 1

If you're playing with a bass player, a typical comping pattern for this tune might be the one shown in Example 2. Note that the chords are played in four-note voicings spread between both hands. The chords are played in root position and they are played in a syncopated fashion, with the second chord of each bar falling on the "and" of beat 2. Also, make sure to leave space on beat 4 in each bar.

EXAMPLE 2

Example 3 offers an alternative pattern. Here, the chords are played as rootless chord voicings in five-note chords. This assumes that you are playing with a bass player.

EXAMPLE 3

TRACK 47
0:21
CD 2

"Bird Blues" hardly sounds like blues, but it is still a viable style. It would be good to familiarize yourself with the "Bird Blues" pattern.

Rhythm changes refers to the chord progression used in George and Ira Gershwin's song "I Got Rhythm," one of the most popular standards from the golden age of the 1930s. The same chord progression has been used in numerous other jazz compositions, including Thelonious Monk's "Rhythm-a-Ning," "Charlie Parker's "Anthropology," and the TV theme "Meet the Flintstones." This is not a 12-bar blues progression, but it is sometimes played by blues musicians as a basis for improvisation. (It's often played by jazz musicians as such.)

Rhythm changes has a 32-bar AABA form, with each section being eight bars. The progression is usually played in B♭, the original key of "I Got Rhythm." The entire progression is given here.

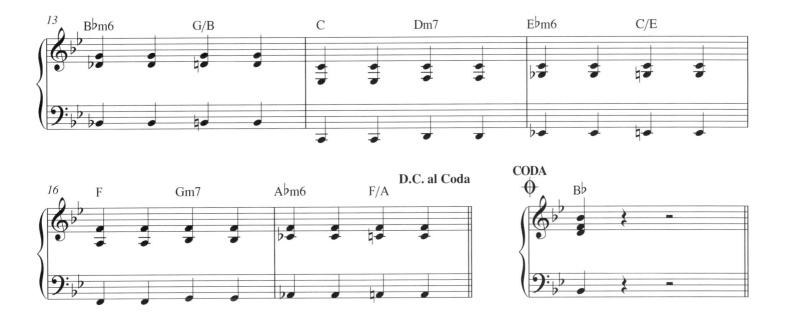

There are many ways that the progression is played. Often substitute chords are used.

Having worked your way through the lessons in this book, you should be able to figure out both one-handed and two-handed comping patterns for the chords. When you perform this with a bass player, you want to leave the bass notes to the bassist and play rootless chord voicings. Think of the lessons involving tritones and their extensions and you can construct chord voicings.

The bridge, beginning with the D chord, is so commonly used in jazz and pop standards, that it is known as the "Sears-Roebuck Bridge." (Perhaps today it should be called the "Walmart Bridge.")

Familiarize yourself with rhythm changes. You never know when you might be called upon to play them.

LESSON #99: THE BO DIDDLEY BEAT

Bo Diddley (Ellas Otha Bates, 1928–2008) was a singer, guitarist, and songwriter who was one of the originators of rock 'n' roll. The **Bo Diddley Beat** was his signature beat. It's essentially a five-accent clave rhythm. Bo Diddley didn't invent the rhythm – it derives from African music, but retains his name nevertheless.

The rhythm can be written out over two bars, as shown Example 1. I usually think of the beat as using two chords, I and IV, but it doesn't have to have a particular harmonic component.

EXAMPLE 1

The beat can also be written in the space of one bar, as in Example 2

EXAMPLE 2

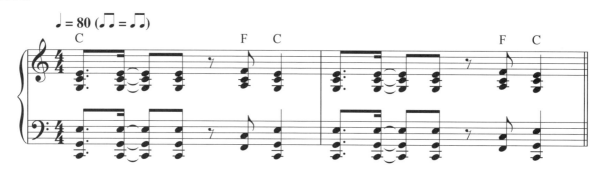

The Bo Diddley Beat has been the basis for many pop songs, including "Not Fade Away" (Buddy Holly), "Willie and the Hand Jive" (Johnny Otis), "I Want Candy" (The Strangeloves), and "Faith" (George Michael). The beat can be used in conjunction with a 12-bar blues pattern.

Alternatively, the beat is often played simply as a groove. Example 3 is an eight-bar excerpt in the manner that Dr. John might play the beat – using just two chords, I and V7.

EXAMPLE 3

LESSON #100: BLUES IN ODD TIME SIGNATURES

The idea for this lesson occurred to me after I accompanied a singer who performed the song "Long as You're Living." The tune has been recorded by many jazz vocalists, from Abbey Lincoln to Karrin Allyson. The lyrics are thoughtful and philosophical. And musically, the song is a 12-bar blues **in 5/4 time**.

It got me thinking, "Why aren't there more blues in odd time signatures?" Obviously, we have 4/4, slow blues in 12/8, and the occasional blues waltz. But why not 5/4 or some other time signature? Blues is harmonically simple, so why not make it more complicated rhythmically?

There are famous songs written in 5/4 time: "Take Five," "The Mission Impossible Theme," and "Everything's Alright" (from *Jesus Christ Superstar*). But 5/4 time is underappreciated, even though it swings, feels natural, and has a nice groove.

5/4 time is usually performed with a particular two-handed accompaniment rhythm:

EXAMPLE 1

I discovered that you can adapt the "All Blues" bass line and chord pattern and play it in 5/4:

EXAMPLE 2

5/4 can also be played with a left-hand accompaniment figure:

EXAMPLE 3

A blues melody in 5/4 might work out somewhat like this:

EXAMPLE 4

Once I started thinking about 5/4, I thought some more. What about a blues in 6/4? So I came up with the following groove. I believe it would work well played in a 12-bar blues.

EXAMPLE 5

Then I thought about Dave Brubeck, a pioneer of odd time signatures and I came up with this groove in 7/4 time:

EXAMPLE 6

The point of all this is to think of blues as something that doesn't have to be stock, ordinary, routine or automatic. Be brave. Be bold. You don't have to play in 4/4 all the time.

PLAY PIANO LIKE A PRO!

AMAZING PHRASING – KEYBOARD
50 Ways to Improve Your Improvisational Skills
by Debbie Denke
Amazing Phrasing is for any keyboard player interested in learning how to improvise and how to improve their creative phrasing. This method is divided into three parts: melody, harmony, and rhythm & style. The companion CD contains 44 full-band demos for listening, as well as many play-along examples so you can practice improvising over various musical styles and progressions.
00842030 Book/CD Pack $16.95

BEBOP LICKS FOR PIANO
A Dictionary of Melodic Ideas for Improvisation
by Les Wise
Written for the musician who is interested in acquiring a firm foundation for playing jazz, this unique book/CD pack presents over 800 licks. By building up a vocabulary of these licks, players can connect them together in endless possibilities to form larger phrases and complete solos. The book includes piano notation, and the CD contains helpful note-for-note demos of every lick.
00311854 Book/CD Pack $16.99

BOOGIE WOOGIE FOR BEGINNERS
by Frank Paparelli
A short easy method for learning to play boogie woogie, designed for the beginner and average pianist. Includes: exercises for developing left-hand bass • 25 popular boogie woogie bass patterns • arrangements of "Down the Road a Piece" and "Answer to the Prayer" by well-known pianists • a glossary of musical terms for dynamics, tempo and style.
00120517 .... $7.95

INTROS, ENDINGS & TURNAROUNDS FOR KEYBOARD
Essential Phrases for Swing, Latin, Jazz Waltz, and Blues Styles
by John Valerio
Learn the intros, endings and turnarounds that all of the pros know and use! This new keyboard instruction book by John Valerio covers swing styles, ballads, Latin tunes, jazz waltzes, blues, major and minor keys, vamps and pedal tones, and more.
00290525 .... $12.95

JAZZ PIANO VOICINGS
An Essential Resource for Aspiring Jazz Musicians
by Rob Mullins
The jazz idiom can often appear mysterious and difficult for musicians who were trained to play other types of music. Long-time performer and educator Rob Mullins helps players enter the jazz world by providing voicings that will help the player develop skills in the jazz genre and start sounding professional right away — without years of study! Includes a "Numeric Voicing Chart," chord indexes in all 12 keys, info about what range of the instrument you can play chords in, and a beginning approach to bass lines.
00310914 .... $19.95

101 KEYBOARD TIPS
Stuff All the Pros Know and Use
by Craig Weldon
Ready to take your keyboard playing to the next level? This book will show you how. *101 Keyboard Tips* presents valuable how-to insight that players of all styles and levels can benefit from. The text, photos, music, diagrams and accompanying CD provide an essential, easy-to-use resource for a variety of topics, including: techniques, improvising and soloing, equipment, practicing, ear training, performance, theory, and much more.
00310933 Book/CD Pack $14.95

OSCAR PETERSON – JAZZ EXERCISES, MINUETS, ETUDES & PIECES FOR PIANO
Legendary jazz pianist Oscar Peterson has long been devoted to the education of piano students. In this book he offers dozens of pieces designed to empower the student, whether novice or classically trained, with the technique needed to become an accomplished jazz pianist.
00311225 .... $12.99

PIANO AEROBICS
by Wayne Hawkins
Piano Aerobics is a set of exercises that introduces students to many popular styles of music, including jazz, salsa, swing, rock, blues, new age, gospel, stride, and bossa nova. In addition, there is a CD with accompaniment tracks featuring professional musicians playing in those styles.
00311863 Book/CD Pack $19.99

PIANO FITNESS
A Complete Workout
by Mark Harrison
This book will give you a thorough technical workout, while having fun at the same time! The accompanying CD allows you to play along with a rhythm section as you practice your scales, arpeggios, and chords in all keys. Instead of avoiding technique exercises because they seem too tedious or difficult, you'll look forward to playing them. Various voicings and rhythmic settings, which are extremely useful in a variety of pop and jazz styles, are also introduced.
00311995 Book/CD Pack $19.99

THE TOTAL KEYBOARD PLAYER
A Complete Guide to the Sounds, Styles & Sonic Spectrum
by Dave Adler
Do you play the keyboards in your sleep? Do you live for the feel of the keys beneath your fingers? If you answered in the affirmative, then read on, brave musical warrior! All you seek is here: the history, the tricks, the stops, the patches, the plays, the holds, the fingering, the dynamics, the exercises, the magic. Everything you always wanted to know about keyboards, all in one amazing key-centric compendium.
00311977 Book/CD Pack $19.99

HAL•LEONARD®
7777 W. BLUEMOUND RD. P.O. BOX 13819
MILWAUKEE, WISCONSIN 53213

Prices, contents, and availability subject to change without notice.

www.halleonard.com

1112

NOTE-FOR-NOTE KEYBOARD TRANSCRIPTIONS

These outstanding collections feature note-for-note transcriptions from the artists who made the songs famous. No matter what style you play, these books are perfect for performers or students who want to play just like their keyboard idols.

ACOUSTIC PIANO BALLADS
16 acoustic piano favorites: Angel • Candle in the Wind • Don't Let the Sun Go Down on Me • Endless Love • Imagine • It's Too Late • Let It Be • Mandy • Ribbon in the Sky • Sailing • She's Got a Way • So Far Away • Tapestry • You Never Give Me Your Money • You've Got a Friend • Your Song.
00690351..$19.95

THE BEATLES KEYBOARD BOOK
23 Beatles favorites, including: All You Need Is Love • Back in the U.S.S.R. • Come Together • Get Back • Good Day Sunshine • Hey Jude • Lady Madonna • Let It Be • Lucy in the Sky with Diamonds • Ob-La-Di, Ob-La-Da • Oh! Darling • Penny Lane • Revolution • We Can Work It Out • With a Little Help from My Friends • and more.
00694827..$22.95

CLASSIC ROCK
35 all-time rock classics: Beth • Bloody Well Right • Changes • Cold as Ice • Come Sail Away • Don't Do Me like That • Hard to Handle • Heaven • Killer Queen • King of Pain • Layla • Light My Fire • Oye Como Va • Piano Man • Takin' Care of Business • Werewolves of London • and more.
00310940..$24.95

JAZZ
24 favorites from Bill Evans, Thelonious Monk, Oscar Peterson, Bud Powell, Art Tatum and more. Includes: Ain't Misbehavin' • April in Paris • Autumn in New York • Body and Soul • Freddie Freeloader • Giant Steps • My Funny Valentine • Satin Doll • Song for My Father • Stella by Starlight • and more.
00310941..$22.95

JAZZ STANDARDS
23 classics by 23 jazz masters, including: Blue Skies • Come Rain or Come Shine • Honeysuckle Rose • I Remember You • A Night in Tunisia • Stormy Weather (Keeps Rainin' All the Time) • Where or When • and more.
00311731..$22.95

THE BILLY JOEL KEYBOARD BOOK
16 mega-hits from the Piano Man himself: Allentown • And So It Goes • Honesty • Just the Way You Are • Movin' Out • My Life • New York State of Mind • Piano Man • Pressure • She's Got a Way • Tell Her About It • and more.
00694828..$22.95

BILLY JOEL FAVORITES KEYBOARD BOOK
Here are 18 of the very best from Billy: Don't Ask Me Why • The Entertainer • 52nd Street • An Innocent Man • Lullabye (Goodnight, My Angel) • Only the Good Die Young • Say Goodbye to Hollywood • Vienna • and more.
00691060..$22.99

ELTON JOHN
20 of Elton John's best songs: Bennie and the Jets • Candle in the Wind • Crocodile Rock • Daniel • Don't Let the Sun Go Down on Me • Goodbye Yellow Brick Road • I Guess That's Why They Call It the Blues • Little Jeannie • Rocket Man • Your Song • and more.
00694829..$22.95

ELTON JOHN FAVORITES
Here are Elton's keyboard parts for 20 top songs: Can You Feel the Love Tonight • I'm Still Standing • Indian Sunset • Levon • Madman Across the Water • Pinball Wizard • Sad Songs (Say So Much) • Saturday Night's Alright (For Fighting) • and more.
00691059..$22.99

KEYBOARD INSTRUMENTALS
22 songs transcribed exactly as you remmember them, including: Alley Cat • Celestial Soda Pop • Green Onions • The Happy Organ • Last Date • Miami Vice • Outa-Space • Popcorn • Red River Rock • Tubular Bells • and more.
00109769..$19.99

ALICIA KEYS
Authentic piano and vocal transcriptions of 18 of her best-known songs, including: Fallin' • How Come You Don't Call Me • If I Ain't Got You • No One • Prelude to a Kiss • Wild Horses • A Woman's Worth • You Don't Know My Name • and more.
00307096 ....$21.95

THE CAROLE KING KEYBOARD BOOK
16 of King's greatest songs: Beautiful • Been to Canaan • Home Again • I Feel the Earth Move • It's Too Late • Jazzman • (You Make Me Feel) Like a Natural Woman • Nightingale • Smackwater Jack • So Far Away • Sweet Seasons • Tapestry • Way Over Yonder • Where You Lead • Will You Love Me Tomorrow • You've Got a Friend.
00690554..$19.95

POP/ROCK
35 songs, including: Africa • Against All Odds • Axel F • Centerfold • Chariots of Fire • Cherish • Don't Let the Sun Go Down on Me • Drops of Jupiter (Tell Me) • Faithfully • It's Too Late • Just the Way You Are • Let It Be • Mandy • Sailing • Sweet Dreams Are Made of This • Walking in Memphis • and more.
00310939..$21.95

R&B
35 R&B classics: Baby Love • Boogie on Reggae Woman • Easy • Endless Love • Fallin' • Green Onions • Higher Ground • I'll Be There • Just Once • Money (That's What I Want) • On the Wings of Love • Ribbon in the Sky • This Masquerade • Three Times a Lady • and more.
00310942..$24.95

ROCK HITS
30 smash hits transcribed precisely as they were played. Includes: Baba O'Riley • Bennie and the Jets • Carry On Wayward Son • Dreamer • Eye in the Sky • I Feel the Earth Move • Jump • Layla • Movin' Out (Anthony's Song) • Tempted • What a Fool Believes • You're My Best Friend • and more.
00311914 ....$24.99

STEVIE WONDER
14 of Stevie's most popular songs: Boogie on Reggae Woman • Hey Love • Higher Ground • I Wish • Isn't She Lovely • Lately • Living for the City • Overjoyed • Ribbon in the Sky • Send One Your Love • Superstition • That Girl • You Are the Sunshine of My Life • You Haven't Done Nothin'.
00306698..$21.95

Visit Hal Leonard online at
www.halleonard.com

Prices, contents and availability subject to change without notice.
0213

HAL•LEONARD KEYBOARD PLAY-ALONG

The **Keyboard Play-Along** series will help you quickly and easily play your favorite songs as played by your favorite artists. Just follow the music in the book, listen to the CD to hear how the keyboard should sound, and then play along using the separate backing tracks. The melody and lyrics are also included in the book in case you want to sing, or simply to help you follow along. The audio CD is playable on any CD player. For PC and Mac users, the CD is enhanced so you can adjust the recording to any tempo without changing pitch! Each book/CD pack in this series features eight great songs.

1. POP/ROCK HITS
Against All Odds (Take a Look at Me Now) • Deacon Blues • (Everything I Do) I Do It for You • Hard to Say I'm Sorry • Kiss on My List • My Life • Walking in Memphis • What a Fool Believes.
00699875 Keyboard Transcriptions $14.95

2. SOFT ROCK
Don't Know Much • Glory of Love • I Write the Songs • It's Too Late • Just Once • Making Love Out of Nothing at All • We've Only Just Begun • You Are the Sunshine of My Life.
00699876 Keyboard Transcriptions $12.95

3. CLASSIC ROCK
Against the Wind • Come Sail Away • Don't Do Me like That • Jessica • Say You Love Me • Takin' Care of Business • Werewolves of London • You're My Best Friend.
00699877 Keyboard Transcriptions $14.95

4. CONTEMPORARY ROCK
Angel • Beautiful • Because of You • Don't Know Why • Fallin' • Listen to Your Heart • A Thousand Miles • Unfaithful.
00699878 Keyboard Transcriptions $14.95

5. ROCK HITS
Back at One • Brick • Clocks • Drops of Jupiter (Tell Me) • Home • 100 Years • This Love • You're Beautiful
00699879 Keyboard Transcriptions $14.95

6. ROCK BALLADS
Bridge over Troubled Water • Easy • Hey Jude • Imagine • Maybe I'm Amazed • A Whiter Shade of Pale • You Are So Beautiful • Your Song.
00699880 Keyboard Transcriptions $14.95

7. ROCK CLASSICS
Baba O'Riley • Bloody Well Right • Carry on Wayward Son • Changes • Cold As Ice • Evil Woman • Space Truckin' • That's All.
00699881 Keyboard Transcriptions $14.95

8. BILLY JOEL – CLASSICS
Angry Young Man • Captain Jack • Honesty • Movin' Out (Anthony's Song) • My Life • Only the Good Die Young • Piano Man • Summer, Highland Falls.
00700302 Keyboard Transcriptions $14.99

9. ELTON JOHN BALLADS
Blue Eyes • Candle in the Wind • Daniel • Don't Let the Sun Go Down on Me • Goodbye Yellow Brick Road • Rocket Man (I Think It's Gonna Be a Long Long Time) • Someone Saved My Life Tonight • Sorry Seems to Be the Hardest Word.
00700752 Keyboard Transcriptions $14.99

10. STEELY DAN
Aja • Do It Again • FM • Hey Nineteen • Peg • Reeling in the Years • Rikki Don't Lose That Number.
00700201 Keyboard Transcriptions $14.99

11. THE DOORS
Break on Through to the Other Side • Hello, I Love You (Won't You Tell Me Your Name?) • L.A. Woman • Light My Fire • Love Me Two Times • People Are Strange • Riders on the Storm • Roadhouse Blues.
00699886 Keyboard Transcriptions $15.99

12. CHRISTMAS HITS
Baby, It's Cold Outside • Blue Christmas • Merry Christmas, Darling • Mistletoe and Wine • Santa Baby • A Spaceman Came Travelling • Step into Christmas • Wonderful Christmastime.
00700267 Keyboard Transcriptions $14.95

13. BILLY JOEL – HITS
Allentown • Just the Way You Are • New York State of Mind • Pressure • Root Beer Rag • Scenes from an Italian Restaurant • She's Always a Woman • Tell Her About It.
00700303 Keyboard Transcriptions $14.99

14. LENNON & McCARTNEY
All You Need Is Love • Back in the U.S.S.R. • Come Together • Get Back • Good Day Sunshine • Hey Jude • Penny Lane • Revolution.
00700754 Keyboard Transcriptions $14.99

15. ELVIS PRESLEY
All Shook Up • A Big Hunk O' Love • Blue Suede Shoes • Can't Help Falling in Love • Don't Be Cruel (To a Heart That's True) • I Want You, I Need You, I Love You • Jailhouse Rock • Love Me.
00700755 Keyboard Transcriptions $14.99

16. 1970s ROCK
Dream On • Highway Star • I Feel the Earth Move • Foreplay/Long Time (Long Time) • Point of Know Return • Sweet Home Alabama • Take the Long Way Home • Will It Go Round in Circles.
00700933 Keyboard Transcriptions $14.99

17. 1960s ROCK
Gimme Some Lovin' • Green Onions • I'm a Believer • Louie, Louie • Magic Carpet Ride • Oh, Pretty Woman • Runaway • The Twist.
00700935 Keyboard Transcriptions $14.99

18. 1950s ROCK
Blueberry Hill • Good Golly Miss Molly • Great Balls of Fire • The Great Pretender • Rock and Roll Is Here to Stay • Shake, Rattle and Roll • Tutti Frutti • What'd I Say.
00700934 Keyboard Transcriptions $14.99

19. JAZZ CLASSICS
Blues Etude • (They Long to Be) Close to You • Freeway • Lonely Woman • My Foolish Heart • Tin Tin Deo • Watch What Happens.
00701244 Keyboard Transcriptions $14.99

20. STEVIE WONDER
Boogie On Reggae Woman • Higher Ground • I Wish • Isn't She Lovely • Living for the City • Sir Duke • Superstition • You Are the Sunshine of My Life.
00701262 Keyboard Transcriptions $14.99

21. R&B
Baby Love • Easy • For Once in My Life • I Can't Help Myself (Sugar Pie, Honey Bunch) • I Heard It Through the Grapevine • Mess Around • Respect • Respect Yourself.
00701263 Keyboard Transcriptions $14.99

22. CAROLE KING
I Feel the Earth Move • It's Too Late • Jazzman • (You Make Me Feel Like) a Natural Woman • So Far Away • Sweet Seasons • Will You Love Me Tomorrow (Will You Still Love Me Tomorrow) • You've Got a Friend.
00701756 Keyboard Transcriptions $14.99

23. WORSHIP
Above All • Be unto Your Name • Beautiful One • Here I Am to Worship • I Give You My Heart • We Fall Down • Wonderful Maker • Worthy Is the Lamb.
00701930 Keyboard Transcriptions $14.99

HAL•LEONARD® CORPORATION
7777 W. BLUEMOUND RD. P.O. BOX 13819
MILWAUKEE, WISCONSIN 53213

www.halleonard.com